"Why hasn't a boo[k] ... The church could hav[e] ... the wisdom contained [in these pages had been] available. Even though we are asked to be 'fools for Christ's sake,' we are not to be foolishly deceived.

"I am so glad that my friend, John Williams, has exposed some of our gullibility so that we can avoid some of the traps we have fallen into. We are to be 'wise as serpents and harmless as doves,' but in many ways, we have been neither.

"John's style of writing makes this book a joy to read while we learn from our mistakes. I believe you will be very glad you read this book."

DR. JOHN BENEFIEL, TH.D.
Senior Pastor, Church on the Rock, Oklahoma City,
and Chairman, the Oklahoma Concert of Prayer

"Trust me! No, don't trust me. . . . Read this book and you will be greatly blessed with the wisdom and wit of John Williams. It is a book that will become a favorite in your library and all of your friends'. Williams is 'right on the mark' about deception in this new and insightful book about the church—a must-read for all pastors, lay leaders, and friends who need to know the difference between what is 'God's Truth' and the world's idea of 'knowledge.' I will be waiting for John Williams' next book, eagerly."

DR. KEN PEARCE, PH.D.
Associate Professor of Psychology
California Baptist University, Riverside

"When I first heard of this book being written, I thought, *It's about time!* What a great need for the church! As long as I've been a Christian, the spiritual 'rumor mill' has been active and effective in eroding the credibility of the church and the testimonies of those who claim Christ as their Lord.

"In a day and time when the voice of the church needs to have integrity and power, we have let speculations and hoaxes keep us from being effective in our witness. The truth is good enough without embellishment. Thank you, John Williams, for the enjoyable and sometimes witty way in which you have uncovered these areas and helped us to see the truth."

DAVID A. SMITH
Executive Pastor, Calvary Assembly,
Winter Park, Florida

THE
COST
of
DECEPTION

THE
COST
of
DECEPTION

THE SEDUCTION *of* MODERN
MYTHS AND URBAN LEGENDS

JOHN A. WILLIAMS

BROADMAN
& HOLMAN
PUBLISHERS

NASHVILLE, TENNESSEE

0-8054-2381-8

Published by Broadman & Holman Publishers,
Nashville, Tennessee

Library of Congress Catalog Number: 00-068089

1 2 3 4 5 6 7 8 9 10 05 04 03 02 01 00

To the memory of my father and mother.
Thank you for your example.

To my wife Jane and daughters Rachel and Rebekah.
Thank you for your love.

To our dear friends Jim, Becky, and Ashley.
Your friendship has kept us through the storms.

To all the Board of Reference of the Oklahoma Concert of Prayer.
With your prayers and effort we will see all of Oklahoma saved
and transformed.

CONTENTS

→ ←

Foreword		xi
Introduction		1
1.	Legends in Our Own Minds	13
2.	Christian Urban Legends	22
3.	The Petition That Won't Go Away	37
4.	Entertaining Angels	46
5.	Busting Hell Wide Open	57
6.	The Missing Day	63
7.	As Seen on TV	71
8.	Be Afraid, Be Very Afraid	79
9.	The Misinformation Age	96
10.	The Experts Speak	113
11.	Millennium Fever	121
12.	The End of the World	136
13.	Will the Real Antichrist Please Stand Up?	156
14.	Y2K—the Bug That Didn't Bite	174
15.	Onward Christian Soldiers	194
	Appendix	201
	Notes	203

FOREWORD

➤ ✦

The church needs a book like this every few years. Perhaps there will be sequels from the same pen. It is certainly welcome wisdom to rumor-weary believers.

God alone can accurately assess damage and ridicule to the Christian cause and the needless waste of time incited by undiscerning reaction to continuing fables. A casual observation of recent, as well as not-so-recent, Christian history presents a body of convincing evidence that points to carelessly sounded false alarms, tales unworthy of retelling, and blind naïveté.

The Christian landscape is strewn with the litter of ill-based hopes and unfounded expectations promoted by well-intentioned pilgrims as well as a few intentional frauds and deceivers. It is time for the Christian world to "catch on"!

What a TIME . . . ly book! With the turn of the calendar to 2000 and all the scenarios predicted for pandemonium possibilities, this could be a time- and face-saving device for thinking believers everywhere. Hopefully and happily this word may be a cure to long-standing naïveté, a caution against repeating stories with no documentation, and an encouragement to steer clear of fables, tales, and folk stories. May it be used as a handbook of rumors we need to avoid repeating and a challenge for us to be done with lesser things and plunge into what is at hand . . . the Kingdom of God!

Thanks, John Williams, for a totally unique approach to a completely common problem!

Lord, deliver us from the gullibility of the curious to a passionate hunger for the Eternal Word of God!

JACK TAYLOR
Dimensions Ministries
Melbourne, FL

INTRODUCTION

➜ ❖ ❖

By early 1999 the first symptoms of "millennium fever" were already causing great agitation in America. The voices of the prognosticators, prophets, and even the profiteers were predicting unimaginable global catastrophes to occur on January 1, 2000. Each vision of what might happen when the clock struck twelve on New Year's Eve was more gloomy, if not frightening, than the one before. Their scenarios of Y2Khaos only fed the uncertainty and alarm in the hearts and minds of an already shaky society.

As early as March 1998, Ed Yourdon, computer consultant and coauthor of the book *Time Bomb 2000,* sensed where there is smoke, there must be fire. He announced, "The Y2K 'fire' has not broken out yet, though we'll begin seeing the first few flames in 1999, possibly as early as January 1, 1999. But like many of my Y2K colleagues, I can already smell the smoke, and I believe, deeply and sincerely, that it's going to be a very bad fire indeed."[1]

So convinced of an impending disaster, Yourdon four months later packed up and moved from New York, explaining, "I recently sold our New York City apartment and bought a house in a small town in New Mexico. . . . I've often joked that I expect New York to resemble Beirut if even a subset of the Y2K infrastructure problems actually materialize—but it's really not a joke. . . . Y2K is sufficiently worrisome, in my opinion, that I'll make sure my family isn't there when the clock rolls over to January 1, 2000."[2]

By February 1999, Yourdon daringly predicted, "We're going to suffer a year of technological disruptions, followed by a decade of depression. We're likely to be living in an environment much like the Third World countries some of us have visited, where nothing works particularly well."[3]

If there were any who put their confidence in software providers' abilities to find a fix for the Y2K bug, they may have been disheartened when Microsoft's own chief technical officer, Nathan Myhrvold, told *Fortune* magazine that these doomsday forecasts couldn't simply be dismissed. "It's very hard to tell how bad the situation will be. I'm sure things will break. It's very hard to dispel a nightmare scenario . . . . The dark-side scenario of airplanes falling out of the sky and bank computers crashing is possible. But it's fundamentally very, very hard to know whether the impact will be big or little."[4]

Even information from a special congressional committee in Washington offered little hope. In a bipartisan report on the Year 2000 computer problem released in March 1999, Senators Robert Bennett of Utah and Christopher J. Dodd of Connecticut held, "[Y2K is a] worldwide crisis, one of the most serious and potentially devastating events this nation has ever encountered. . . . The interdependent nature of technology systems makes the severity of possible disruptions difficult to predict. . . . Make no mistake, this problem will affect us all individually and collectively in very profound ways. . . . It will indeed impact individual businesses and the global economy. In some cases, lives could even be at stake. . . . Those who suggest that it will be nothing more than a 'bump in the road' are simply misinformed."[5]

Though the initial warnings of a Y2K crash were secular in origin, some Christian spokesmen found a way to cast the looming problem in a religious light. Gary North, a Christian Reconstructionist and head of The Institute for Christian Economics, urged Christians to quit their jobs, buy gold and grain, and find a remote cabin safe from all of the rioting sure to come. North warned, "We've got a problem. It may be the biggest problem that the modern world has ever faced. I think it is. At 12 midnight on January 1, 2000, most of the world's mainframe computers will either shut down or begin spewing out bad data. Most of the world's desktop computers will also start spewing out bad data. Tens of millions—possibly hundreds of millions—of pre-programmed computer chips will begin to shut down the systems they automatically control. This will create a nightmare for every area of life, in every region of the industrialized world."[6]

Since 1996, North's website warned of catastrophic troubles ahead concerning the Y2K bug. North added, "In all of man's history we have never been able to predict with such accuracy a worldwide disaster of this magnitude. The millennium clock keeps ticking. There is nothing we can do."[7]

Other prominent Christian leaders saw the Y2K problem as a forerunner to the apocalypse. In an August 1999 sermon broadcast on his *Old Time Gospel Hour* from Lynchburg, Virginia, pastor Jerry Falwell predicted God's wrath on January 1, 2000. His ministry distributed a packet called "The Y2K Time Bomb," including a video, "A Christian's Guide to the Millennium Bug," advising the faithful to be prepared for disaster. "Y2K is God's instrument to shake this nation, to humble this nation," Falwell said. "He may be preparing to confound our language, to jam our communications, scatter our efforts, and judge us for our sin and rebellion for going against his Lordship."[8]

Christian Broadcasting Network founder and author Pat Robertson was also marketing a video called "Preparing for the Millennium: A CBN News Special Report," which summarized both the Y2K problem and Robertson's novel, *The End of an Age*, in which Armageddon is triggered by a meteorite crash.

In early 1998, Tim LaHaye and Jerry Jenkins, authors of the best-selling *Left Behind* series of books about the Apocalypse, predicted large-scale turmoil on January 1, 2000. The Y2K bug could trigger "financial meltdown," warned LaHaye, "making it possible for the Antichrist to dominate the world."[9]

Through various Christian media, sermons, tapes, and books, believers were urged to stock up on dried food, water, and in some cases, even weapons to help their families survive. The more enterprising left their jobs to sell preparedness packages, generators, and survival kits. Advertisements in Christian magazines promoted gold and silver coins as a hedge against a stock market computer malfunction and a worldwide depression. At The Prophecy Club, a Kansas-based publishing house, customers with $1,400 could purchase enough dehydrated food to feed four people for a year.

At "end time" prophecy conferences, gold and silver coins were snapped up to the tune of $1.75 million as a hedge against a doomsday economic crash according to Kevin DeMeritt, president of Lear Financial Incorporated in Santa Monica, a gold seller at these conferences.

Thomas L. Clark, a member of the Forest Preserve Bible Church, considers himself an "informed fundamentalist." He runs an online Internet business called Y2K Prepare that sells food mills and a survival dome, and offers tips on how to store food and water in case of calamity. Clark claims one raw-grain firm was back-ordered eight months on some products, and he expected there would be too great a demand to meet it all by the end of 1999. Clark says online articles from those predicting disaster convinced him that there would be no silver bullet arriving in time. "Everybody thinks *they* are going to fix it. But who are *they*?"[10]

Due to the heightened apprehension, a growing number of apocalyptic books and videos were feverishly being turned out. Titles like *Final Mysteries Revealed, Planet Earth: The Last Chapter,* and Michael Hyatt's *The Millennium Bug: How to Survive the Coming Chaos,* were hard to keep in stock. As the year

2000 approached, Christian retail outlets reported a sharp rise in the sale of biblical prophecy books, especially those by authors who tied Y2K with apocalyptic themes such as the Antichrist's rise to power, Armageddon, and the rapture of the church. Books like *Y2K=666* enjoyed brisk sales in many Christian bookstores.

A fictional novel by Richard Wiles, *Judgment Day 2000,* featured a character resembling Bill Gates as a type of Antichrist. The story depicted how the breakdown of all computers caused America to be vulnerable to terrorists with nuclear bombs hidden in suitcases. Wiles, once a marketing director for the Christian Broadcasting Network, believes God directed him to write his book. "In 12 months we'll know if I'm right," he says. "If I'm wrong, the worst that will happen to me is I'll be tremendously embarrassed. If other people are wrong and don't listen to me, the worst that will happen is all men will perish."[11]

Yet, in the face of all this unsettlement, many families like the Eckharts of rural Lisbon, Ohio, were showing great resolve in the midst of what one doomsayer predicted to be "the biggest problem the modern world has ever faced." Bruce, an automation technician for Daimler-Chrysler, his wife Diane, and their eleven-year-old daughter Danielle were self-confident not just from the purchase of a gas-powered home generator in case of massive power outages, or the year's supply of dehydrated food in their basement, but from their decision to buy a waterbed for Danielle. Among those concerned about a Y2K collapse, the loss of public utilities was one of the biggest fears. So they purchased the waterbed so that, if necessary, they would have three hundred gallons of water on hand. "I hope we don't end up drinking my bed," Danielle said.[12]

Since 1997 the Eckharts had been stockpiling food, converting their savings into gold coins, and perfecting their firearm skills. Just in case those who were caught unaware came looking for food, the Eckharts also had two rifles, a shotgun, and a handgun. "I know I don't have to fear the future," said Diane. "I only worry about people who aren't prepared."[13]

In case of a medical emergency, Diane learned rudimentary dentistry and field medicine. "I want to be able to stitch a wound and fill a cavity," she said.[14]

The Eckharts were not alone in preparations for a possible worldwide meltdown of our computer systems, public utilities, and financial system. Tim Chambers, the pastor of the 250-member Christ Church in Joplin, Missouri, said, "There are some people who are making preparations for the end of the world, as we know it—or at least a long interruption. It has the potential to be divisive, and, initially, there have been relationships that were put under some measures of strain."[15]

"There won't be any accidental survivors," said Bryan Elder, who was a marketing major at the University of Arkansas and ran a hydraulics service company until he began studying biblical prophecies a few years ago. "Hell starts January 1, 2000, when the lights go out."[16] Elder is planning to live in a cave near Cassville, Missouri, that can accommodate 125 people for as long as seven years. Elder believed that an alignment of the planets in May 2000, along with a nuclear war and a solar windstorm, would burn up the earth.

Others, however, were more optimistic about the coming chain of events. Landon Mosley, an Ohio steelworker who claimed to be preparing for the Lord's return by stockpiling food and reading at least one prophecy book a month says, "It's really a rejoicin' time, seeing the return of Jesus Christ!"[17]

When New Year's Eve arrived, Bruce and Diane Eckhart awoke at 4:30 A.M. and turned on their two televisions and shortwave radio, for what they believed could be the last time, to monitor the first Y2K rollover in Kiribati. "So far, it's just a minor power outage in New Zealand," Diane noticed.

As the year 2000 emerged across the rest of the world, there were no significant reports of loss of utilities, blackouts, or computer failures. Not even countries that were considered to be behind in fixing Y2K were having any problems. Danielle seemed to be the first family member to face reality. "We won't have to go grocery shopping for a while," she said. While Bruce was still wary of looters from neighboring Youngstown, Diane was already contemplating what to do with their huge supply of canned goods. "I'm going to save on groceries," she says. "I can't decide if I'm going to buy a Jacuzzi or a new computer with the money."[18]

Cynics could easily dismiss those who made extraordinary predictions about a Y2K global disaster as foolish. Better-mannered people would call them misguided. Whatever the case might be, as the new millennium approached, both the prophets and promoters were in high gear. Powered by the mystery of a new millennium and fueled by an apocalyptic event like Y2K, those who preached "the end is near" found a receptive audience among millions of American Christians.

In the aftermath of a Y2K washout, the most important question we must ask ourselves is this: How could so many people, who were so earnest in their convictions, be so wrong? Similarly, why has the American church been so brazen in predicting the date of the Rapture, the return of Christ, and naming the Antichrist, only to be proven wrong again and again? What is it that causes us to be so easily deceived? If the church is to be known as " the pillar and support of truth" (1 Tim. 3:15), we must learn to see how our pessimistic predictions concerning Y2K may have caused us to lose face in a world desperately needing the one who is the truth.

To withdraw from the concerns of the world, waiting for God to destroy the earth, while we hide safely out of harms way, is giving Christianity (and ultimately Christ) a bad name. Astonishing as it may seem to those outside the faith, a number of the faithful actually appeared heartened by the bad news, believing that bringing an end to life as we know it on this planet is prelude to the coming kingdom of God. While passively waiting for the soon return of the Lord Jesus Christ, we may be unconsciously neglecting the Great Commission—to go into the entire world and preach the gospel of Christ. It gives the perception that if the end is just around the corner, why bother. Worse yet, erroneous expectations and false predictions have made us look foolish and irresponsible to a world that needs direction.

When looking back at the different Christian perspectives on the Y2K crisis, the irony is how profoundly many Christian evangelicals and fundamentalists had been influenced not only by the Word of God, but also by information coming from the secular media. Mainline Protestants and Catholics, for the most part, maintained that reason as well as revelation was needed in facing the challenges as we entered a new millennium. As Christians we have a responsibility to not only speak but also demonstrate the truth. Our words—and to a greater degree, our actions—make a statement about how we see our world. Before we make specific claims about the future, we should carefully consider the accuracy and truthfulness of our information. This calls for discernment and sound judgment, and confronting our world prudently, with the utmost humility, always holding God's Word as the truth.

As the church is "the pillar and support" or foundation of truth, we as the individual pillars must faithfully uphold and consistently portray the truth of God's word in a world very much at enmity with him. To do this effectively, believers cannot live in deception and compromise in our private lives, then attempt to communicate and demonstrate the truth to others.

It is for this reason that Paul spends the third chapter of 1 Timothy describing the character and attributes all believers should pursue. He speaks that Christian leaders should be blameless, vigilant, sober, of good behavior, not violent or greedy for money, and "holding to the mystery of the faith with a clear conscience" (1 Tim. 3:9).

Then Paul states, "Although I hope to come to you soon, I am writing you these instructions so that, if I am delayed, you will know how people ought to conduct themselves in God's household, which is the church of the living God, the pillar and foundation of the truth" (1 Tim. 3:14–15 NIV).

God needs pillars of integrity to represent him in this world. He will only build his work on the foundation of men and women who are not only eager to know the truth, but equally zealous to live and communicate the truth to those who are ignorant. This crucial truth is found in the very next verse: "And without controversy great is the mystery of godliness: God was manifest in the flesh, justified in the Spirit, seen of angels, preached unto the Gentiles, believed on in the world, received up into glory" (1 Tim. 3:16 KJV).

This is the truth we must proclaim to all the earth, that Jesus was more than a good man, more than a teacher or prophet. He is the Savior. He is Emmanuel, "God with us." The sum total of all truth was so much a part of who he is that Jesus said, "I am the truth." Even when he was confronted by Pilate concerning his claim of being a king, Jesus answers, "To this end was I born, and for this cause came I into the world, that I should bear witness unto the truth. Every one that is of the truth heareth my voice" (John 18:37 KJV).

Paul describes the role of the church in two words: the church is the *pillar* and the *foundation* of the truth. One of the reasons for the existence of the church is to introduce truth back into a world inundated with error, with imagination, a world that follows humanistic ideas. We live in a confusing world that is getting more confused all the time.

The church is needed to speak the truth in the midst of that confusion so the world can come to know a loving God. Everywhere, on every side, you find people hungry for this. The cry of the world is, "Who has the answers for our problems?" It is to answer that distressing call that the church has been sent as a light into the darkness of the world. The church is to present the truth when all else seems lost.

As God's ambassadors in this world, we are each called to be extraordinary pillars, upholding the revelation of the truth that enlightens and sanctifies men, making them free indeed.

In order to be "pillars and the support of truth" in this world, the church must first win the battle that is as old as the Garden of Eden. Satan is a deceiver and is still working to disqualify

Christians from their right to be heard. The beloved apostle John saw Satan in his apocalyptic vision as the great dragon who "was thrown down, the serpent of old who is called the devil and Satan, who deceives the whole world" (Rev. 12:9). Satan is not yet bound in hell for eternity but is like a roaring lion seeking those he can devour (see 1 Pet. 5:8). Our need in this day is to be wary of his tactics of deception and to expose his works of darkness. With God's grace, we can stop our enemy from disqualifying our lives and our testimony. Like Samson, we can tear down the pillars in people's minds that hold up a worldwide "temple of satanic deception."

In this information age where knowledge abounds and where the Internet can spread a myth or legend at the "speed of lies," we must become more prudent in our assessment of the truth. It is crucial that our testimony to the world not be tainted with exaggeration, fabrication, or fear. Deception can also come from those outside sources that by nature are deceptive. There are people looking for believers who are young and immature or who have been spiritually offended and have become weak. Jesus warned his disciples of such men when he said, "See to it that no one misleads you" (Matt. 24:4).

In spite of the many good uses of the Internet, there is no system for testing the validity of what is available online. Everyone has an equal voice, no matter how mistaken the information may be. In the World Wide Web without end, all opinions seem to have the same weight and value. The Internet makes no distinction between information and values. By contrast, Christianity has always insisted that knowledge is worthless without a moral and cultural context. This context helps us judge between the holy and the profane, the worthless and the worthwhile, while gaining knowledge and wisdom.

There is a lot of hooey that has been given validity by the replication and forwarding of urban legends and e-mail myths. Perhaps you've recently signed a petition to stop an atheist's effort to ban shows like *Touched by an Angel*. Most of us have been told about the computer in Belgium called "The Beast" that has a record of every living human being. Even our pulpits are not immune from perpetuating urban legends. Have you ever heard during a wedding ceremony that as a result of the creation of the first woman, all men have one less rib than women? Ask any doctor; men have the same number of ribs as women. These myths still persist today despite the fact they are not true.

Paul wrote to his son in the faith, Timothy, about faithfulness to God's abiding truth. In his first letter Paul encouraged him to, "instruct certain men not to teach strange doctrines, nor to pay attention to myths and endless genealogies, which give rise to mere speculation rather than furthering the administration of God which is by faith" (1 Tim. 1:3–4).

With so much at stake in the new millennium and the prospects of a Y2K global shutdown never materializing, today is a day when Christians need godly wisdom. Instead of blindly accepting the bad report of the day and burying our heads, we should be sharpening and deepening the message of hope and reconciliation to a dying and rapidly decaying world.

To do this we must first understand how hoaxes, urban legends, and false predictions, as well as our own gullibility, have affected our proclamation of the gospel of truth. We must learn how to recognize the popular legends, myths, and fallacies that litter our cultural landscape.

Mark Twain once wrote, "A lie can travel halfway around the world before the facts have even put their boots on." My hope is that this book will, at the least, expose the fables being promoted as truth in the kingdom of God and, at best, put his sheep in a position of rest.

Let us determine to not grow weary or faint in our desire to uphold God's truth. There is a wonderful promise to the "pillars" living in this present age who are determined to endure to the end: "He who overcomes, I will make him a pillar in the temple of My God, and he will not go out from it anymore; and I will write upon him the name of My God, and the name of the city of

My God, the new Jerusalem, which comes down out of heaven from My God, and My new name.

"He who has an ear, let him hear what the Spirit says to the churches" (Rev. 3:12–13).

CHAPTER ONE

Legends in Our Own Minds

→ ←

Urban legends are best described as popular tales that usually involve some combination of off-the-wall, humorous, frightening, or supernatural events. They almost always happen to someone else, like a friend of a friend or a distant cousin from a previous marriage once removed. Many of them remind us of stories we heard as children around a campfire or at a slumber party, or as adults around the office. The storyteller assures us that the tale "really" happened and provides just enough detail to make the story enjoyable and believable. Often there seems to be a moral to the story, like "watch out, be warned, or this could happen to you."

Urban legends have been told by well-known commentators like Paul Harvey and have appeared in letters to both Dear Abby and her sister Ann Landers. Many times after hearing them you would almost swear you heard that same story on the news or read it in the paper.

Like the tall tales of legendary characters such as Paul Bunyan and Pecos Bill, these stories were originally passed down by the lost art of storytelling. But with the advance of the World Wide Web, e-mail, and fax machines, these urban legends are now more quickly spread and at an exponential rate. Urban legends are rarely traceable to a single source and often seem to spring out of nowhere. Odds are that you've heard, received, or sent copies of some of the numerous urban legends circulating via the Internet.

CASE STUDIES

Barbara Mikkelson and her husband, David, operate the Urban Legends Reference Pages Web site. They gather, examine, and often debunk reports that are widely circulated on the Net. "They're sometimes honest mishearings of current news items, which are transmuted and then embellished by every recipient," Barbara explains. "What someone thought they heard becomes 'fact,' and there is at least a faint aura of plausibility. Nowadays, it takes no effort. It arrives already packaged and ready to go—you just send it off to 20 of your friends."[1]

I remember the first urban legend I heard as a young boy. It was about a deranged criminal with a stainless steel hook in place of his right hand who terrorizes young couples parked in lover's lane. As the story goes, a young couple hears a news bulletin on the radio about his escape from a local insane asylum. Suddenly they hear scratching noises coming from the front passenger side of the car. Immediately the boy fires up the engine and peels away toward the safety of the city lights. As the young man arrives at his date's house, he pulls into the driveway, then goes around the back of the car to open her door, and there, hanging from the door handle, he sees a stainless steel hook!

For years there have been rumors of alligators lurking in New York City's sewer system. As this urban legend goes, vacationers to Florida who brought back baby alligators as pets, end up flushing them away when the gators begin to grow too large and cumbersome to keep. Supposedly the gators grew to an enormous size deep in the dark underground of the Big Apple and reportedly have resurfaced through sanitation pipes, attacking unsuspecting homeowners. Nature writer Diane Ackerman doubts that alligators could handle such an environment. "They couldn't survive for any length of time in the sewers, only a few months at the most, because they can't live long in salmonella or shigella or E. coli, organisms that one usually finds in sewage. Also, alligators live at temperatures between 78 and 90 degrees." Despite a lack of verifiable news reports on actual alligator-in-the-sewer sightings, this urban legend still persists to this day.[2]

Another classic urban legend is known as "the solid cement Cadillac." According to the story, a cement-truck driver is on his way home for lunch and is surprised to see a new Cadillac convertible standing in his driveway. He parks his truck some distance away, sneaks up to the kitchen window, and sees his wife talking to a strange man. Suspecting that his wife is having an affair, the driver backs his truck up to the Caddy and dumps a full load of wet concrete into it.

That evening, when he comes home from work, he finds his wife in tears as she watches the Cadillac being towed away. In hysterics by now, she tells her husband how the car dealer had delivered the new car she had bought for his birthday. She had been saving for years to buy him his dream car.

Folklorist Jan Harold Brunvand, who dubbed this next legend "The Hare Dryer," notes that it was extremely popular in America during the late eighties. On two separate occasions in 1989, this legend was told as a "true story" by celebrity guests on *The Tonight Show with Johnny Carson*.

According to the story, a man walked into his garden one day to find his dog holding the lifeless body of the neighbor's prize rabbit in its mouth. Although no obvious injury could be seen, the rabbit was very dead.

The horrified man initially panicked, but then came up with a brilliant scheme. He took the rabbit inside, shampooed and blow dried it, and then quickly snuck next door to put it back in its hutch before the neighbor got home.

A few days went by and he heard nothing from his neighbor. Then on the following weekend the man saw his neighbor working in the backyard. As they began talking over the fence, his neighbor said that a strange thing had happened to him that week. When he came home from work one night he found his prize rabbit dead in its hutch.

"Oh, no," the man said. "How awful!"

"That's not the strange part," explained the neighbor. "What's odd is that it had died earlier that morning, and I buried it before going to work!"

Usually around the Christmas shopping season you hear "reports" of a slasher who lies in wait under shoppers' cars at a local mall. When they approach carrying their holiday packages, he reaches out from under the car and cuts their ankles with a knife. When the shopper falls to the ground, he crawls out from under the car, grabs the packages, and runs away.

In 1989, this rumor was so pervasive that a mall in Tacoma, Washington, had to set up police field stations around its parking lot to calm the customers who were too frightened to do their holiday shopping.

In another urban legend that is tinged with terror, a woman entered the emergency room with an inflamed neck apparently caused by an allergic reaction to snakebite. The woman recalled feeling a sharp pain in her neck when she put on her new winter coat the previous day.

The coat, it seems, was made in some South American country, and investigators found a small snake sewn inside the lining.

The snake had somehow managed to bite the woman through the material.

Another variation of the story has a woman shopping for coats at Kmart. She puts her hand in one of the pockets and feels a sharp prick. When she takes her hand out she notices blood on her finger. She presumes it was just a straight pin left in the pocket, and doesn't think more about it. The next morning she becomes violently ill and is rushed to the hospital where it is discovered she has been bitten by a poisonous snake.

If that's not enough to make you jumpy, consider this story concerning a young couple that noticed their newly delivered mattress seemed rather lumpy when they lay down to sleep. After a fitful first night, the couple decided the mattress was defective and returned it to the retailer. The store couldn't understand why it was so lumpy, so they tore the mattress apart. Evidently during production in yet another South American country, a live anaconda was accidentally sewn in the mattress.

Here's a story a friend of mine told me "really" happened. One summer morning a young woman is on her way to a nearby supermarket to pick up some groceries. As she is about to enter the store she notices an elderly woman sitting in her car, the windows rolled up, her eyes closed, and both hands behind the back of her head. Being a nurse, the young woman becomes concerned and walks over to the car. She notices that the woman looks strange and isn't moving at all. She asks the elderly woman if she is OK, and the woman faintly replies that she's been shot in the back of the head and has been holding her brains in for more than an hour.

The nurse quickly calls the paramedics, who break into the passenger side of the car because the doors are locked and the woman refuses to remove her hands from her head. When they finally get in, they find that the elderly woman has a wad of bread dough hanging on the back of her head.

Apparently a canister of Pillsbury biscuit dough in her grocery sack in the back had exploded from the heat, making a sound like a gunshot, and a gob of dough hit her in the back of her head. When she reached back to find out what it was, she felt the dough and thought it was her brains, which she bravely tried to hold in until someone noticed and came to her aid.

Despite my friend's earnestness, this story, which has been around since the mid-90s, was completely untrue. Nevertheless, it has found new life on the Internet. Comedienne Brett Butler has even used it as a part of her stand-up comedy routine.

According to another story, many have been privileged to learn the secret recipe of the Neiman-Marcus Cookie. As the story goes, a woman and her daughter had finished sharing a salad at the Neiman-Marcus department store cafe in Dallas and decided to have dessert. Being cookie lovers, they decide to try the "Neiman-Marcus Cookie." The woman was so taken by the cookie she asks if the girl at the counter would give her the recipe. The girl refuses, saying, "We don't give out our recipes." The woman asks if she can buy the recipe? The girl at the counter says with a smile, "Sure. Why not." Asking how much it costs, the girl replies, "Two fifty." The woman charges it on her credit card.

Thirty days later, she receives her VISA statement from Neiman-Marcus and it totals $285.00. Checking the statement she remembers she and her daughter had only spent $9.95 for two salads and about $20.00 for a scarf. The bottom of the statement read, "Cookie Recipe—$250.00." Upset, the woman calls Neiman's accounting department to complain that when the waitress said "two fifty," she believed that meant $2.50 for a cookie recipe.

When the store refuses to refund her money, the woman plots her revenge. She not only mails and faxes the recipe to all of her friends with a note to copy and send this to as many people as they can, but she posts the "secret" recipe on the Internet for all to see.

It's a great story, but I heard it was the recipe for Mrs. Fields' cookies. Others have heard it was a recipe from a famous restaurant for their red velvet cake, or a secret fudge recipe.

BATTLING URBAN LEGENDS
WITH SCRIPTURE

What these urban legends have in common are that they are fun or shocking to tell, entertaining to hear, and simply not true. Except in a few cases, it is usually impossible to determine the origin of Internet legends: they reappear every few months or years in slightly different versions, travel through cyberspace, and then disappear. Whether they are forwarded by e-mail or passed along by word of mouth, these messages can clog company computers, create mistrust, and encourage foolish behavior.

Because of the explosion of the World Wide Web, our interpersonal communication is shrinking. So is it any surprise that mistrust and suspicion are on the rise? How can we trust others if we haven't taken the time to know them? It's no wonder these hoaxes and myths have the power to deceive us as our society becomes more and more fragmented. Christians must guard themselves from the distrust and suspicion that can destroy community.

As a young boy, there was an excitement about swapping these fables with others and wondering about the truth behind each tale. It was a time of sweet innocence, wonderment, and awe. However, today as an adult and a pastor, I am constantly amazed at the gullibility of some Christians to readily accept urban legends with no thought as to their accuracy.

In 1998 I delivered a sermon called "The Attack of the Fifty-Foot Choking Doberman Traveling with the Vanishing Hitchhiker Using a Noncompliant Y2K Computer." My intent was to expose many of the most popular Christian urban legends and show how they cloud our thinking concerning the world around us. At that time I was concerned not only about urban legends but also about the many scenarios being touted by well-meaning Christians regarding the year 2000 and the Y2K bug.

Thousands of new users sign onto the Internet for the first time every day of the week. I can tell by the hundreds of free

America Online membership disks that I've collected for coasters. These new users are usually unaware of the potential for deception and are vulnerable to misinformation. As the Net grows, so does the number of hoaxes and pranks carried by e-mail. Barbara Mikkelson says, "Rumors, pranks, and hoaxes are not unique to the Internet, but they spread more quickly because of it."[3]

Looking to the "Spirit of Truth," the Holy Spirit will keep us balanced whenever we show a tendency to fall into error. In Ephesians 1:17, Paul refers to the Holy Spirit as "a spirit of wisdom." It follows that those who are under his direction and influence should be "children of wisdom." We should strive for this sensitivity to the Spirit of wisdom daily. If we only listen to those around us, we may not only miss who God wants us to be but also miss golden opportunities to share truth when myths and legends are being spread.

As we read in Proverbs 8:12, wisdom and prudence go hand in hand. God has made Christ abound toward us "in all wisdom and prudence" (Eph. 1:8 KJV), implying at the same time that he has called us to become "the wise and the prudent."

Proverbs 14:8 says, "The wisdom of the prudent is to understand his way, But the folly of fools is deceit." A prudent person carefully considers all circumstances and consequences, never acting rashly or foolishly. The prudent show good judgment and discernment in their actions and words, demonstrating sound wisdom and discretion.

Just as worldly wisdom takes up its dwelling in the unregenerate minds of lost men and women, God's heavenly wisdom takes up its residence in the regenerated hearts of the redeemed. Proverbs 14:33a says, "Wisdom rests in the heart of one who has understanding."

We must strive to hold fast to the truth. As the sheep of his pasture, we should not allow ourselves to be easily fleeced. It will take persevering leaders and strong, faithful witnesses to accomplish God's work in the coming years. We must be wise and discerning amid this information-addicted generation.

Concerning the need for the church to "make a good appearance," the apostle Paul's encouragement to the church at Philippi applies to us today: "Do all things without grumbling or disputing; that you may prove yourselves to be blameless and innocent, children of God above reproach in the midst of a crooked and perverse generation, among whom you appear as lights in the world" (Phil. 2:14–15).

CHAPTER TWO

Christian
Urban Legends
→ ←

S top me if you've heard this one.

A doctor tells a patient that he must undergo a dangerous brain transplant. The patient asks the doctor what types of brains are available.

"Well, for $5,000 I could give you the brain of a noted physicist," the doctor replied. "Or for $10,000 I could let you have the brain of a university professor. But I also have the brain of a Christian. It goes for $50,000."

"Why so much for the Christian's brain?" the man asks.

The doctor answered, "Because it's never been used."

Most humor has an element of truth in it; that's what makes it so funny. Proverbs 14:15 says, "A simple man believes anything, but a prudent man gives thought to his steps" (NIV).

CASE STUDIES—"THE MARK"

You may have heard about a frightening rumor that the U.S. government has accidentally issued checks containing some alarming instructions. A California prophecy teacher, Charles Taylor, helped spread this particular story in a tract his ministry issued. In part it states: "Scores of Social Security checks were accidentally mailed to recipients that required a special and unusual process for cashing. It was so unusual that banks refused to even try to cash them. The instructional paragraph of these particular checks was changed to read that the party cashing the check MUST HAVE THE PROPER IDENTIFICATION MARK IN THEIR RIGHT HAND OR FOREHEAD."

Taylor further claimed, "From Florida to Washington to California, I have reports of almost 100 persons who received the 'forehead or hand' Social Security checks." However, when questioned later, Taylor said, "I haven't seen an actual check, no. I have talked to people in the realm of rumor. I've talked to people about it, but I haven't actually seen one."[1]

When I heard the story for the first time back in the eighties, the conclusion was that one recipient called the local Social Security office to inquire about the peculiar guidelines. The employee at the other end of the line told her there had been a mistake. He said, "Those checks aren't supposed to be released till next year. Please send that one back."

It didn't make sense to me that a government program as volatile as the Social Security System would be printing checks a year in advance. No one has ever produced one of these "mark of the beast" Social Security checks or even a photocopy; yet this story is still being shared in Christian circles as true.

I recently received an e-mail that had been copied and forwarded to many others concerning a frightening event at a Wal-Mart discount store. It seems a woman in the checkout line was shocked when she noticed the man in front of her paying for his purchase. As the cashier told the man the total of his purchase, he held out his right hand, and the cashier passed the scanning device over it. The amount of the purchase was credited to the register and the man picked up his bags and walked out. Stunned as she approached the cashier, the woman asked about the transaction. The cashier replied, "Oh yes. We're one of a handful of stores experimenting with debit chips embedded in customer's hands. We expect it to be in place by next year."

Embedded chips, futuristic commerce, a nationally recognized chain involved! Could all of these be leading to a one-world government and a new worldwide money system using embedded chips in our hands and foreheads? The fact is, the story is not true. There has never been any documented proof as to the location of the store or who originated the story. While the technology does exist to embed medical information chips in someone's hand, we are still a long way as a society from accepting this as a way of doing business.

Some Christian urban legends can make us believe that anything from a corporate conspiracy to an ultraliberal faction are secretly working with the antichrist to hinder, if not stop altogether, the work of God in America. So, armed with only what we've heard, we respond by boycotting, marching, signing petitions, or calling those responsible, only to find out we've been duped. Such hoaxes can erode our integrity, truly making us fools for Christ.

THE MIKE HUTCHINSON STORY

Take for instance the story of missionary Mike Hutchinson. Many churches have responded to a plea to pray for God to spare his life. This plea has appeared in e-mail correspondence, prayer chains, and church newsletters across the U.S. Here is a copy of the e-mail message I received in January 2000.

Fwd: prayer request and health warning

Mike Hutchinson and his family, I.M.B. missionaries in Guinea-Bissau, West Africa, need our prayers. His car was surrounded by Muslims as he and his family drove home. After patiently waiting and asking them to move, they finally pulled away from his car. As Mike started to drive away, a 16-year-old Muslim jumped (or was pushed) in front of Mike's car and was killed. The Muslims arrested Mike (took his passport) and are placing him on trial for murder. If convicted, he will be hanged immediately. His wife, Lynn, and his children (12, 10, 9) are staying with another missionary family. Please pray for God's intervention. Please share this with your church, prayer chain, e-mail list and anyone else you know who will pray for this missionary.

Fortunately, according to information supplied by the International Mission Board and the First Baptist Church of Long Beach, California, only part of this e-mail message is true. Hutchinson was involved in an auto accident on April 30, 1999, in which a teenage boy was killed, but the rest is myth. The local authorities treated Hutchinson's case routinely and properly, and he was never in danger of being lynched. At last report, missionary Mike Hutchinson is alive and well, and has returned to the United States to take up a ministry closer to home.

In a newsletter dated November 1999, Mike Hutchinson himself issued this statement:

Many of you have heard of my car accident in Senegal. A young Senegalese boy was killed in this accident. Lynn and I did all we could to get him to medical help in time, but to no avail. We reported directly to the police and began the legal process that takes place in Senegal whenever such things happen. The police, and since then, the people involved in their judicial system, have treated me fairly and shown us every considera-tion. My travel was tightly controlled for months, but that has been lifted. I still await a possible trial if the judge feels it is necessary. Many of you have received false information that a mob had gath-ered around us or that I was being hung. Neither could be further from the truth.[2]

For several months after the accident, letters asking for inter-cession on his behalf have traveled around the world. How this story spun out of control is not certain, but it points out how unreliable Christian urban legends can be when we don't have all the facts.

ALASKA AIRLINES FLIGHT 261

Another legend making the Internet rumor rounds concerns the fateful flight of Alaska Airlines Flight 261 that went down off the coast of California on January 31, 2000. On March 24, 2000, I received an e-mail containing a message that was intended to demonstrate God's ability to turn a tragedy into a triumph. This is a copy of the letter:

Alaska Airlines Flight 261

John H. (a friend of ours at church) recently shared testimony that is so remarkable, and credi-ble, that we feel compelled to share it with a wider audience. John related that last week he talked with an Alaska Airlines pilot who is involved in the investigation of the horrific crash of Alaska Flight 261.

The pilot has listened to the cockpit voice recorder from the downed plane, and he reported that for the last 9 minutes of the flight, the wife of the pastor from Monroe, Washington, can be heard sharing the Gospel with the passengers over the plane's intercom system. Just before the final dive into the Pacific Ocean, she can be heard leading the sinner's prayer for salvation.

The pilot also reported that the flight data recorder from the plane indicates that there is no good explanation for how the plane was able to stay in the air for those final 9 minutes. But it did stay in the air until the pastor's wife had a chance to share the Gospel with the very attentive passengers and presumably lead many to salvation in Christ.

So, in the midst of this tragedy, nearly 90 people had an extraordinary opportunity to get right with their Maker just prior to meeting Him.

After reading the message, I quickly sent a reply back to the person who forwarded the story to me, asking if they could verify who had originated the story in the first place. They later supplied me with the name and e-mail address of the person, so I sent that person a message asking if they could identify the John H. in the story, and the name and location of the church where this allegedly took place. They never could verify where this happened or who initially told them this tale.

What could be a tremendous testimony of faith looks as if it's merely a Christian urban legend. The couple that perished in the crash was later identified as Joe and Linda Knight, copastors of The Rock Church in Monroe, Washington. They were returning from a humanitarian trip to Puerto Vallarta, Mexico, when the Alaskan airliner went down.

The legend may have grown out of a statement made to reporters by the couple's son. In a story published in the *Seattle Post—Intelligencer*, reporter James Wallace wrote, "No one will ever know exactly what happened aboard the flight. But sources close to the federal crash investigation said the cockpit voice recorder did not pick up any final prayer."[3]

Wallace said, "In interviews with reporters after the crash, Jeff Knight, the family's son, said he was sure his mother would have been standing in the aisle during the plane's last moments, preaching and helping frightened people find God.

"'A lot of people met Jesus that day through my mom,' he was quoted as saying."[4]

Only God knew the condition of the hearts of those people, and it would be wonderful to believe that he had placed one of his own in a strategic position that day. All we do know for sure is that God is merciful and desires that none should perish. Our only hope is in him, not in a legend.

THE "HOMOSEXUAL JESUS" FILM

Maybe you've heard from friends or read in a Christian newsletter that an upcoming film will portray Jesus as a homosexual and will costar a notorious French prostitute. Here is a copy of the actual petition that has been distributed for several years:

> Modern People News has revealed plans for the filming of a movie based on the SEX LIFE OF JESUS in which Jesus is portrayed as a swinging HOMOSEXUAL. This film will be shot in the U.S.A. this year unless the public outcry is great. Already a French prostitute has been named to play the part of Mary Magdalene, with whom Christ has a blatant affair. We CANNOT AFFORD to stand by and DO NOTHING about this disgrace. We must not allow this perverted world to drag our Lord through the dirt. PLEASE HELP us to get this film banned from the U.S.A. as it has been in Europe. Let us show how we feel.
>
> Detach and mail the form below to the address

shown. Make a few copies and give them to your friends. Only one name per copy.

Dear Attorney General Scott,

I would like to protest, in the strongest terms possible, the production, filming, and showing of any movie that supposedly depicts the sex life of JESUS CHRIST by MODERN PEOPLE NEWS, 11030 West Addison Street, Franklin Park, Illinois 60181.

Such a movie would be blasphemous and would be an outrage and contrary to the truth. We urge you to take proper action against this moral corruption.

This story's origin dates as far back as 1984. By the end of 1985 more than a million Christians had written protest letters in an attempt to get this fictitious film banned. In other variations, the name of the publication the story is taken from is Modern Film News, and the protest letters are directed to the Attorney General of either Illinois or Alabama. Other versions of the petition have added this attachment: "Evangelist Jimmy Swaggart recently reported that the above-mentioned movie has been completed!!! According to Brother Swaggart, the movie company has released word that the movie is scheduled to be shown in various locations around the country during the Christmas season. So, the time is short to put a stop to it. We sincerely hope that all spiritually and morally minded people will band together and keep this ungodly type of filth out of Alabama."

In his book *The Mexican Pet,* Jan Brunvand discovered that in Gadsen, Alabama, "radio station personnel had attempted to contact Modern People News and had been in touch with the Alabama attorney general's office. Following these efforts at verification, a statement was read on the air saying that although the attorney general had received between two and three thousand letters over a period of several weeks concerning the supposed gay-Jesus movie, no evidence could be found that such a project ever existed. Modern People News, it was stated, seemed to have either gone out of business or changed their name."[5]

In January 1985, advice columnist Ann Landers, ran a letter from the attorney general's office of Illinois that tried to set the record straight. Here is the letter that appeared in her daily column:

Dear Ann Landers:

The office of the Attorney General of the State of Illinois respectfully requests your assistance in combating an international chain letter that is distressing hundreds and thousands of Christians and those of other faiths as well.

The chain letter is a plea to protest "in the strongest possible language" the making of a movie in which Jesus Christ could be depicted as a swinging homosexual. Both this office and the Associated Press have chased down every possible clue and cannot find a shred of truth in the story that such a film was ever in production.

Modern Film News, which reported the film plans, has been out of business for more than two years. Moreover, 90 percent of the protest mail that has been overwhelming our staff is addressed to the former attorney general, William J. Scott, who has been out of office longer than four years.

Despite our efforts to get the word to the public that the chain letter is a hoax, we continue to receive approximately 1,000 protests every week and at least a dozen phone inquiries each working day. The inquiries and protests have come from 41 states, Canada, Puerto Rico, New Zealand, Australia, Cambodia, Spain, Brazil, the

Dominican Republic, India, the Philippines, Guatemala, Costa Rica and Portugal.

We have concluded that the "Jesus movie" rumor originated in 1977 when a suburban Chicago publication, Modern People News, reported that certain interests in Europe were planning such a film and requested that readers express their opinion of the purported project. The result was the chain-letter protest, which, for some unknown reason, has been revived and is again sweeping the world.

We are appealing to you, Ann Landers, to help us get the word out. The scope of your readership and impact on millions of newspaper readers around the world cannot be overestimated.

The postage and phone calls, not to mention the valuable time of employees, run into a great deal of money that could be used for so many worthwhile purposes. Will you please help us?

Neil F. Hartigan, Attorney General, State of Illinois

Ann's reply to Hartigan's plea was short and to the point, saying:

Dear Attorney General Hartigan:

Hoaxes die hard and the zanier the hoax, the more difficult it is to convince people that it is not true.

If any of you, my readers, receive a copy of that wacky chain letter, take my word for the fact that there is not an iota of truth in it. And please tell friends that chain letters are illegal and should be tossed into the handiest wastebasket or fed to the nearest goat.[6]

THE "BEAST" IN BELGIUM

At some point in their life, almost every Christian has heard the story about a large computer, reportedly three stories tall, somewhere in Belgium that has the ability to track every living man, woman, and child on earth. It is known by the rather ominous name, "the Beast." This Christian urban legend has been taught and preached from the smallest Sunday school to the largest pulpit, but the facts in this story are the stuff of science fiction.

The Beast was supposedly designed to give every person on earth a unique ID number, to be placed on the forehead or the back of the hand by either laser or embedded chip. This "mark of the beast" or as some imagine, a bar code, will work with scanners in every place of business and will be necessary for buying and selling in the near future.

In 1979 prophecy teacher Colin Deal helped popularize the alleged computer in his book *Christ Returns by 1988—101 Reasons Why*. Quoting an "expert" source, Deal claimed the computer is capable of assigning a number to every person on earth in the form of a laser tattoo.

Several years earlier, the Southwest Radio Church covered the same story. They first reported in 1966 that a computerized, cashless society was coming, and in 1975 Southwest stated that a "Beast" computer system was being constructed that "would connect banks in Canada, the Common Market, and the USA." In a 1977 newsletter article on this "Beast" system, Southwest said, "What we are projecting here is a socialistic economic leveling and a new money system in the 1980s."[7]

Writer Rich Buhler in his collection of urban myths featured on *The Ship of Fools* Web site, said, "There are various printed versions of the story that date back to 1973, but the most widely circulated early account appeared in *Christian Life* magazine in August 1976."

Three months after publishing the story of the Beast, *Christian Life* received a letter from Christian author Joe Musser. In it, he explained that the Beast computer of Belgium did not exist at all in reality, but only in fantasy. Musser said that he created the account for a novel he wrote, titled *Beyond a Pale Horse*, and for a screenplay for the David Wilkerson film *The Rapture*. In the letter, Musser said that for three years he had seen the story he had created being passed along by Christians as being true.

The opportunity for confusing fiction with fact was there from the outset. As part of the promotion for the David Wilkerson film, some mock newspapers had been printed that had convincing-looking news stories about events that could be associated with the rapture, including the Beast computer of Belgium. Unless one read the small print next to the copyright notice, there was nothing to indicate that it was fiction.[8]

Think back to what computers looked like in the early seventies. The component space necessary for a computer to store information was the size of a large room. Now, the same component can easily fit in a laptop computer. I only hope that if this is real, the Antichrist has kids, and he can't get any time on "the Beast" to do his work.

With the number of television sets in use growing rapidly in the U.S., and the advent of satellite dishes and digital cable, it was just a matter of time before someone made a connection between "the boob tube" and the Antichrist. Some prophecy teachers are claiming that the Antichrist may be watching us all right now through fiber optics; wiring that sends electronic digital light signals through miniature glass fibers instead of traditional coaxial cable wires.

Emil Gaverluk and Patrick Fisher, in Southwest's 1979 book *Fiber Optics: The Eye of the Antichrist,* said: "There is a pinhead sized camera lens on the end of the fiber optic which can watch anything taking place in the room, including the reactions of the viewers to any specific program. The data is recorded on computers, which can collate all remarks pro, and con, to implement dictatorial control by any group or individual. The startling thing is the fish-eye camera lens can still see and record everything, EVEN WHEN THE TELEVISION SET IS NOT TURNED

ON. This means that every family will be under 24-hour surveillance. What a perfect setup for the Antichrist."

Later in the book, Fisher claimed that computers working in conjunction with "the Beast" computer in Brussels had "already dropped the flag that says, 'Go Now,'" to begin a major Middle East or, possibly, world war.

I wonder why we miss the impracticality of some of these stories. If the beast can track all living beings, how many employees would the Antichrist need just to track and sort all the information? The world would never know unemployment.

BAR CODES AS THE "MARK"

Many Christians over the years have been nervous over the invention and use of the Universal Product Code bar code system. Today, virtually every product you purchase from a grocery store, department store, or mass merchandiser has a UPC bar code on it somewhere. UPC bar codes were originally created to help grocery stores speed up the checkout process and keep better track of inventory, but the system quickly spread to all other retail products because it was so successful.

UPCs originated with a company called the Uniform Code Council (UCC). A manufacturer applies to the UCC for permission to enter the UPC system. The manufacturer pays an annual fee for the privilege. In return, the UCC issues the manufacturer a six-digit identification number and provides guidelines on how to use it.

Barbara Mikkelson reports from her *Urban Legends Reference Pages* that THE EAN-13 bar code system is used in eighty-five countries, making it the most popular of its kind in the world. It works by using thirteen numbers, each one represented by seven vertical lines. The seven lines are either black or white, making a pattern that is recognized as a particular digit when scanned by a computer.[9]

What seems to be sinister about the UPC codes is that every bar code has tiny vertical lines at the beginning, middle, and end.

These three lines, called the guard bars, do not have a particular value but look exactly like the bar code symbol for the number six. Some would mistakenly claim that these three sixes appear on all products. However, if you look closely at a six on a bar code, you will see that there is a wide white bar either to the left or the right (depending on where the number is positioned), which is not the case with the guard bars.

Despite overwhelming evidence that the bar code system is not an evil tool ready to scan our heads at the twelve items or less checkout counter, Reuters news service reported a story about God-fearing Greek Cypriots who were leery of carrying new identity cards. The Island's Greek Orthodox Church sought assurances that the new cards would not bear the so-called "number of the beast," which the Bible's Book of Revelation says will identify the Antichrist.[10]

According to the report, an interior ministry official told Reuters the new cards would, in any case, carry six and not three digits.

In an article published in *Christianity Today,* writer David Neff illustrated how some Christian leaders are playing to the fears of church members in the books they write. "Perhaps most outlandish was a stack of books (we saw at the annual Christian Booksellers Association convention in Orlando, Florida) with the title *Satan-Proof Your Home,* apparently treating the devil as if he were radon gas. Most were more tasteful, yet clearly appealing to readers' self-protective instincts: there were books that played on fear of psychologists, fear of charismatics, fear of twelve-step programs, fear of Antichrist, fear of school-teachers, and fear of New Age influences." This would appear as if Christians are led more by fear than by the Holy Spirit.

A truth-hungry world can be easy to motivate when it sees positive examples in our lives. Paul's counsel to the church at Colossae to "conduct yourselves with wisdom toward outsiders, making the most of the opportunity," seems more appropriate than ever for believer's today (Col. 4:5).

Yet if Christians fall for these myths, our good news can be heard as "the sky is falling." An alarmist reaction to today's news events can result in the world not taking Christians or Christianity seriously. Paul wrote, "Be very careful, then, how you live—not as unwise but as wise, making the most of every opportunity" (Eph. 5:15 NIV). An unwise person does not have a strategy to maximize opportunities to share truth. Consequently, many people never take advantage of opportunities to participate in the growth of Christ's kingdom.

CHAPTER THREE

The Petition That Won't Go Away

→ ←

When Nerlande Louis-Jean learned from an e-mail message that atheists were asking the Federal Communications Commission to ban all religious programming, she took immediate action. As a devout Christian, Nerlande quickly forwarded the enclosed petition to all of her friends in hopes of stopping what she believed amounted to banning God from the airwaves.

The only problem was, the e-mail message was a fraud.

THE DRAMA

When it comes to this classic Christian urban legend, simple arithmetic could save a lot of paper and embarrassment. The first time I heard about the Madalyn Murray O'Hair petition to eliminate all Christian programs and broadcast music was in July 1983. At the time I was working as the program director of a Christian music station in Oklahoma City. That summer the radio station sponsored a Christian Business show for businesses and ministries to display their products, programs, and wares. Two ladies hosted a booth during the show to get signatures on a petition that would reverse a decision pending before the Federal Communications Commission. The copy of their petition had been mimeographed so many times it was washed out and difficult to read. Carefully making out each word I read this:

> Madalyn Murray O'Hair, an atheist, whose effort successfully eliminated the use of Bible Reading and Prayer from public schools fifteen years ago has now been granted a Federal hearing in Washington, D.C., on the same subject by the Federal Communications Commission (FCC). Her petition, P.M. 2493, would ultimately pave the way to stop the reading of the Gospel on the airwaves of America. She took her petition with 287,000 signatures to back her stand. If her attempt is successful, all Sunday worship services being broadcast, either by radio or television, will stop. Many elderly people and shut-ins as well as those recuperating from hospitalization or illness depend on radio and television to fulfill their worship needs every week.
>
> Madalyn is also campaigning to REMOVE ALL CHRISTMAS PROGRAMS, CHRISTMAS SONGS, AND CHRISTMAS CAROLS from public schools. You can help this time! We need

1,000,000 (one million) signed letters. This
should defeat Ms. O'Hair and show that there are
many CHRISTIANS ALIVE AND WELL AND
CONCERNED in our country. This petition is
NUMBER 2493. Sign, cut off and mail the form
below. PLEASE DO NOT SIGN JOINTLY AS
Mr. and Mrs. Let each adult SIGN ONE sepa-
rately and mail it in a separate envelope. BE
SURE TO PUT PETITION NUMBER 2493
ON THE ENVELOPE when mailing your letter.
  Please send this letter out to anyone that can
help in the cause.

The accompanying letter addressed to the FCC said:

  Gentlemen:
  I am an American and proud of my heritage. I
  am also very much aware of the place religious
  faith has played in the freedom we as Americans
  now enjoy. Therefore, I protest any human effort
  to remove from radio and television any programs
  designed to show faith in GOD or a SUPREME
  BEING or to remove CHRISTMAS SONGS,
  CHRISTMAS PROGRAMS, AND CHRISTMAS
  CAROLS from public airwaves, schools, or office
  buildings.
  Sincerely,

  NAME: _____

  ADDRESS: _____

  As I was reading the petition, I began doing some subtracting
in my head. Since the first line of this petition refers to "fifteen
years ago," and the Supreme Court decision affecting school
prayer was in 1963, that meant this petition was written sometime
in 1978.

To give some background on this legend, in the late fifties, Madalyn Murray O'Hair, a recognized atheist, happened to hear students reciting "The Lord's Prayer" at the junior high school her son, Bill Murray, then 14, was attending. In December 1960 her attorneys filed a petition with the Superior Court of Baltimore, Maryland, asking the court to force the board of education to stop the "illegal" Bible reading and prayer exercises. The petition stated, among other things, that Bill's religious liberty was being threatened by placing a premium on belief as against nonbelief. For three years, Bill and Madalyn Murray fought school prayer all the way to the Supreme Court, and on June 13, 1963, they finally won, with a landmark ruling that removed mandatory public school prayer.

By an overwhelming 8-1 vote, the court reversed an earlier Maryland Court of Appeals decision and ruled that the opening Bible reading and prayer exercises were unconstitutional. The majority opinion said in part,

> The place of religion in our society is an exalted one achieved through a long tradition of reliance on the home, the church, and the inviolable citadel of the individual heart and mind. We have come to recognize through bitter experience that it is not within the power of government to invade that citadel, whether its purpose or effect be to aid or oppose, to advance or retard. In the relationship between man and religion, the state is firmly committed to a position of neutrality. The breach of neutrality that is today a trickling stream may all too soon become a raging torrent, and in the words of Madison, "It is proper to take alarm at the first amendment on our Liberties."[1]

As a result, in 1964 *Life* magazine named Madalyn Murray "the most hated woman in America."

The real story of the infamous FCC petition actually began much later, on December 1, 1974. Two small radio operators, Jeremy D. Lansman and Lorenzo W. Milam, frustrated with the difficulty in helping minority groups set up small commercial FM radio stations, filed a "Petition for Rulemaking" with the FCC. One of the three requests made in that petition concerned a request for a "freeze" on all applications by religious, Bible, Christian, and other sectarian schools, colleges, and institutes for FM and TV channels normally reserved for educational organizations. The petition was received by the FCC on December 5, 1974, and clocked into the Rules and Standards Division on December 6, 1974. It was given the file number R.M.-2493.

The third part of Lansman and Milam's petition had nothing to do with banning religious programming, but merely wanted to limit the special considerations and privileges given to religious broadcasting over secular, nonreligious broadcast outlets when considering licenses for educational frequencies. However, within a year a rumor started that Madalyn O'Hair had filed a petition with 27,000 signatures to ban all religious-themed programs including Christmas music.

On August 1, 1975, the FCC had rejected the R.M.-2493 petition, but nonetheless they had received well over 500,000 letters protesting the imaginary "ban on Christian programming" petition during the summer months alone. By 1976 almost five million letters were received, and by May 1982, the FCC had four full-time employees just opening up mail regarding R.M.-2493. Since 1989 the FCC continues to receive about one million petitions a year to fight a phantom foe.

The FCC has placed a press release on their Internet site to try to put this petition to rest. Their memo reads:

> A rumor has been circulating since 1975 that
> Madalyn Murray O'Hair, a widely known self-pro-
> claimed atheist, proposed that the Federal
> Communications Commission (FCC) consider

limiting or banning religious programming. This rumor is not true. It also has been circulated repeatedly that Ms. O'Hair was granted an FCC hearing to discuss that proposal. This too is untrue.

There is no federal law or regulation that gives the FCC the authority to prohibit radio and television stations from presenting religious programs. Actually, the Communications Act (the law that established the FCC and defines its authority) prohibits the FCC from censoring broadcast material and interfering with freedom of speech in broadcasting.

The FCC cannot direct any broadcaster to present, or refrain from presenting, announcements or programs on religion, and the FCC cannot act as an arbitrator on the insights or accuracy of such material. Broadcasters, not the FCC, nor any other governmental agency, have the responsibility for selecting the programming that is aired by their stations.[2]

I broke the news to the ladies at the business show that this petition was a hoax; the story of a ban on Christian programs and music was not true. I told them that the FCC had sent letters to all radio stations denying the rumor. They looked at each other for a moment with expressions of bewilderment and disbelief. An hour later they closed their booth and left.

Like those dear ladies, there seems to be reluctance among some Christians to believe the truth about this legend. To this day, the petition continues to be passed around at churches and religious events. Today, the U.S. Postal Service, in cooperation with the FCC, now automatically throws away any letters addressed to the FCC with "Petition Number 2493" on the envelope. However, a new twist has been added to this old petition that appears to make it sound more up to date. In an e-mail version of this old hoax, this new opening has been added: "All my Christian friends, please read. This is very important. Let's all send the attached letters in hope and prayer we can stop this event from happening once again. Please share this with everyone! We cannot afford to sit back and be passive on this one. This is really shocking; when you read it you'll realize that CBS will be forced to discontinue 'Touched by an Angel' for using the word 'God' in every program."

The rest of the text reads exactly the same as the original. But if the error in dating went unnoticed, then an even greater reason to doubt this hoax exists. Madalyn Murray O'Hair, along with her other son Jon, and her granddaughter Robin, have been missing and presumed dead since 1995. The mystery of their disappearance began on Monday, August 28, 1995, when employees of the American Atheist Organization showed up for work in Austin, Texas. A strange note was taped to the front door. It said in effect that the Murray O'Hair family had been called out of town on an emergency basis and that all paychecks were in the mail. Her son Jon Murray allegedly signed the note. David Van Biema, reporting for *Time* magazine, writes, "Tax returns filed by groups affiliated with American Atheists suggest that Jon took $629,500 of organization money with him. Although Austin police say they have thus far found no evidence of foul play in the family's disappearance, both O'Hair friends and foes have offered scenarios including kidnapping, murder and flight to New Zealand with the funds."[3] No one has seen or heard from them since.

Thankfully, Bill Murray, the same one who had triggered the fight against school prayer some thirty years earlier, has accepted Jesus as his Lord and has become a respected Christian evangelist. In a glimpse of what life was like living with his famed atheistic mother, Bill shares this reflection from an article on his Web site: "My mother was not just Madalyn Murray O'Hair, the atheist leader. She was an evil person who led many to hell. That is hard for me to say about my own mother, but it is true. When I was a young boy of ten or eleven years old, she would come home and brag about spending the day in X-rated movie theaters in downtown Baltimore. She was proud of the fact she was the only woman in the movie house watching this filth. My mother's whole life circulated around such things. She even wrote articles for Larry Flynt's pornographic magazine, *Hustler*. My mother lived in spiritual death as Paul writes: 'But she that liveth in pleasure is dead while she liveth' [1 Timothy 5:6 KJV]."[4]

Although we do not know for sure what really happened to Madalyn Murray O'Hair, there is one thing we do know, she is not lobbying the FCC to forbid Christmas carols in public schools or on radio and TV. Nevertheless, the fact that she has not been seen in public since 1995 has not slowed the steady tide of these petitions.

WHY CHRISTIANS FALL FOR URBAN LEGENDS

Christian researcher Bob Passantino offers several reasons why Christians can be so easily fooled by Christian urban legends:

They fit into our worldview. "[The fact that] something is possible doesn't mean that it is true; and [the fact that] something exists doesn't mean every report we receive of it must be true," Passantino says.

We accept what we're told. "It's not that we don't want to be critical, but we don't always have time to check everything we're told. We forget that finding someone willing to tell us what to think about a certain situation is not the same as finding the right person to tell us what can be verified."

We base our knowledge on common sense. "Often common sense parallels the truth; that is, what we commonly think makes sense. It may even correspond to truth. But common sense is not a trustworthy method to find truth."

We place too much faith in "experts." "We seem to think that truth gets truer if someone important said it, even if that important person has no particular knowledge of that field. Believing an expert without appropriate authority and without corroborating evidence is not a trustworthy way to discern truth."

We believe what makes us feel comfortable. "In other words, we like to spread the idea that Madalyn Murray O'Hair is on a crusade to stamp out Christian broadcasting. It makes us feel good that we are such a threat to atheists like her."[5]

Larry Eskridge, a staff member of the Institute for the Study of American Evangelicals at Wheaton College, agrees with Passantino's analysis of why rumors like the FCC petition hoax seem so real. He explains, "With evangelicals, [the rumors are] told to you by someone that you trust—a member of your church or a neighbor—and they tell you a story that sounds plausible, and you wouldn't think they're lying to you. They're probably not; they're just passing on what they've heard. The thing just gets passed on and on until it's accepted as fact."[6]

Christians aren't alone in becoming susceptible to the seduction of urban legends and myths. All humans can be just as easily afflicted, but believers tend to be more vocal and proactive when confronted with injustice. For example, between 1975 and 1995, the FCC had received more than 30 million pieces of mail protesting R.M.-2493. Yet without exercising discernment and wisdom that also means 30 million people have been fooled by this hoax. This petition simply refuses to die.

Bob Passantino concludes, "Our credibility is on the line. People might think if Christians are stupid enough to fall for this falsehood, maybe early Christians were gullible enough to fall for the resurrection story. In my view, there are consequences."[7]

When the devout believer I mentioned earlier was later presented with documentation that the FCC petition was a hoax, she still wasn't quite convinced. There had to be something there, she insisted. It was on the Internet.

"You never know," she said. "Maybe somebody is trying to cover up something."[8]

CHAPTER FOUR

Entertaining
Angels

➤ ◄

A man is driving on a lonely highway at night when he spots a hitchhiker walking along the road ahead of him. He stops, the hitchhiker gets in the backseat of the car, and they continue along the highway.

As they talk, the subject of conversation turns to the "last days" and the Second Coming of Christ. The hitchhiker then suddenly pronounces, "It's going to happen sooner than you think! Be ready!" At this, he disappears from the car.

The shaken driver calls the police to report the incident. Strangely, the officer at the other end tells him: "Ordinarily, we wouldn't believe you, but you're the fifth person today who has had that same experience."

In 1982 I was working as a disc jockey at a radio station in Oklahoma City when stories of the vanishing hitchhiker hit the news wire. Reports had come in from neighboring Arkansas that state troopers had talked to several people all reporting they had picked up the disappearing messenger. I called the Arkansas Highway Patrol to check the stories out for myself. I talked with a trooper who said he had heard about the stories, but personally had not taken any calls from the distraught drivers. Our radio station did several stories about the vanishing hitchhiker and received calls from listeners who claimed they knew a friend of a friend that it happened to. Was this true or another Christian urban legend?

The vanishing hitchhiker story is one of the best known and most widely shared of Christian urban legends. It has been repeated in sermons and printed in numerous newsletters, magazines, newspapers, and books around the world. Reports of the vanishing hitchhiker have circulated in the United States, Canada, Western Europe, Korea, and most recently in Australia and New Zealand. So widespread is this story that the world-renowned expert on urban legends, Dr. Jan Harold Brunvand, titled one of his best-selling books on urban legends *The Vanishing Hitchhiker*.

This tale can be traced as far back as the 1800s, where a horse-drawn carriage instead of a car picks up the mysterious traveler. There are also versions involving ghostly horseback riders. This legend has mostly been told around late-night campfires along with other ghost stories; however, somewhere along the way it picked up spiritual overtones, and the hitchhiker was changed from a ghost to an angel. There are other hitchhiker stories featuring lost loved ones.

Barbara Mikkelson, from the *Urban Legends Reference Pages*, says there are always common elements in each version of the story: "The teller usually cites specific local streets where the driver picks up the spectral hitchhiker. Sometimes the ghost leaves

a book or scarf in the car, which the bereaved parents then identify as belonging to their lost daughter. Sometimes the driver
spies the hitchhiker's photograph on the family piano, wearing
the party dress in which she died (and which she was wearing
when he picked her up)."

A modern version of the story was popularized in music in
1965. The hit song "Laurie (Strange Things Happen)" by Dickey
Lee told about a teenage girl dressed in a party dress and a
sweater who vanishes after hitching a ride home and is later identified from a picture as the ghost of a girl who died on that same
day years earlier. The unbelieving driver later returns to the ceme-
tery where she is buried and there finds her sweater on her grave,
the same one she was wearing when he picked her up.

Despite increasing numbers of reports of angel sightings,
there has been disagreement about what they may look like, let
alone whether they exist. People have been reporting angelic
encounters for more than three thousand years now. Their
descriptions have ranged from frightening to pleasant, and from
strange to run of the mill. One thing remains certain: angels
remain mysterious creatures.

The Christian belief about their existence, the purposes they
serve, and the way they act is vastly different from the perception
found in modern media and many New Age books. While most
agree that angels are spiritual beings—entities whose existence
cannot be explained scientifically—only God's Word holds the
real truth concerning angels, both confirming their existence and
explaining their ministry to the saints on this earth.

The Bible describes angels as having supernatural strength
and knowledge (2 Pet. 2:11). Though artists over the centuries
have portrayed angels as having wings, rarely is an angel so
described in the Bible. The only exceptions are the descriptions
of the cherubim and seraphim and the "four living creatures"
(Exod. 25:20; Ezek. 1:6; Rev. 4:8).

Angels were present when God created the world, and they
remain at God's side, ready to carry out his every command.

When making themselves visible to human beings, angels consistently appear in human form (Gen. 18:1–2; Dan. 10:18; Zech. 2:1). Most of the time their appearance inspires fear and awe in people (Judg. 13:6; Matt. 28:3–4; Luke 24:4).

Angels are charged with caring for people and serving them in times of need. They can guide and instruct people (Gen. 24:7, 40; Exod. 14:19), protect the people of God (Exod. 14:19–20; Dan. 3:28; Matt. 26:53), relieve hunger and thirst (Gen. 21:17–19; Mark 1:13), and sometimes deliver the people of God from danger (Acts 5:19; 12:6–11).

Many good Christian books have been written over the last few years containing testimonies of purported angelic visitations. Renowned evangelist Billy Graham wrote a book in 1975 called *Angels: God's Secret Agents* that shares the story of an amazing encounter with an angelic being. Graham shares this account from his book:

> Dr. S. W. Mitchell, a celebrated Philadelphia neurologist, had gone to bed after an exceptionally tiring day. Suddenly he was awakened by someone knocking on his door. Opening it he found a little girl, poorly dressed and deeply upset. She told him her mother was very sick and asked him if he would please come with her. It was a bitterly cold, snowy night, but though he was bone tired, Dr. Mitchell dressed and followed the girl.
>
> As Readers' Digest reports the story, he found the mother desperately ill with pneumonia. After arranging for medical care, he complimented the sick woman on the intelligence and persistence of her little daughter. The woman looked at him strangely and then said, "My daughter died a month ago." She added, "Her shoes and coat are in the clothes closet there." Dr. Mitchell, amazed and perplexed, went to the closet and opened the

> door. There hung the very coat worn by the little
> girl who had brought him to tend to her mother.
> It was warm and dry and could not possibly have
> been out in the wintry night.[1]

Sound familiar? Stories about deliverance from danger by angelic intervention are a common theme in most of these Christian accounts.

Today there is a growing market in America for anything having to do with angels. You can find almost anything from books, pendants, ornaments, charms, figurines, and a variety of other angel paraphernalia. They line the shelves of secular, Christian, and New Age bookstores alike.

Television programs like "Highway to Heaven" and "Touched by an Angel" plus the movies *Angels in the Outfield* and *City of Angels* have inspired a renewed interest in angels. Who hasn't enjoyed the Christmas classic *It's a Wonderful Life,* featuring the hapless angel Clarence, who's trying to earn his wings by assisting Jimmy Stewart.

Washington Post religion writer Barbara J. Saffir highlighted the rising awareness in angels in a 1993 article "Under Wing." She pointed out that at that time four of the top ten paperbacks on the *Publisher's Weekly* best-seller list were books on angels. She also reported, "A recent Gallup poll also found that 76% of teenagers believe in angels. More than 1,000 angel enthusiasts belong to angel organizations across the country; and hundreds of angel followers regularly attended angel workshops and conventions in Washington and across the United States."[2]

Why the seemingly universal appeal of angels? Angels are accepted in most of the cultures of the world. Not only do Christians and Jews have records of the angelic hosts, but so do Muslims, Buddhists, and Hindus. Winged figures have been found in primitive Sumerian carvings, Egyptian tombs, and Assyrian reliefs. Angels are found in metaphysical literature dating from ancient times to the present. Perhaps part of their appeal is because there is a desire in every human heart to know God. This desire for fellowship with a supernatural God also includes a curiosity about his angels. With the explosion of interest in angels, there coexists information produced by the Bible and by Satan, the "angel of light." This is why we must look only to God's Word to find what we need to know about angelic activity.

As New Age influences and esoteric beliefs invade our culture, the reality of angels and their role has become distorted. *Angel Times Magazine* explains that its "contributing writers, columnists and story subjects range from Christian to Jewish to Native American to Hindu, and come from all over the world."

"Angels appear to all people, regardless of culture or religion," explains *Angel Times* publisher Linda Vephula. "We see angels as a common denominator among the religions of the world, and focusing on what we have in common rather than our differences will help unite all peoples spiritually."[3]

Another article appearing in *Angel Times* magazine by Neale D. Walsch author of *Conversations with God I and II,* tells readers, "in the name of God, to follow their feelings, reject biblical moral boundaries, and embrace the UN and its global spirituality."[4]

Today's best-selling angel books assure us that guardian angels are indeed watching over us and are here to do our bidding, like a genie out of a bottle. An angel-oriented collection of more than sixty self-help practices, Terry Lynn Taylor's *Guardians of Hope: The Angel's Guide to Personal Growth* is based on the idea that angels can add a sense of fun, love, and adventure to our stressful and fast-paced lifestyle. Angels, Taylor claims, create miracles, make us happy, enhance our creativity, and bring lightness to life's heavy and difficult problems.[5]

Alma Daniel, Timothy Wyllie, and Andrew Ramer, the authors of *Ask Your Angels,* confide, "We were given an angel to help us in the creation and writing of this book." They describe angels as the "social workers of the universe." They give us unsolicited, unconditional love.[6]

In *The Angels within Us,* author John Randolph Price introduced the idea of the twenty-two "angels," or "centers of Living Energy," that he claims exist in everyone. These "centers" supposedly provide all that is needed on a person's journey through life. In the sequel to his best-selling book, *Angel Energy: How to Harness the Power of Angels in Your Everyday Life,* Price says the natural expression of the angels is truth. If we deny the truth, we repress the energy of the angels. But when we fully accept the eternal verities of life, the angels go to work to bring everything up to the divine standard . . . they await only our readiness. Price also claims that angels require our assistance to manifest changes in our lives. They are able to free us from disease and death, loneliness and unfulfillment, lack and limitation, only when we free them.[7]

In clairvoyant psychotherapist Dr. Doreen Virtue's book, *Healing with the Angels: How the Angels Can Assist You in Every Area of Your Life,* the author gives a how-to guide on working with angels to improve your physical, mental, and emotional health. The daughter of a Christian Science spiritual healer, Virtue is a fourth-generation metaphysician who blends psychology, psychic practices, and principles from the New Age "A Course in Miracles" into her counseling practice and writing. She says, "The angels are here to teach us that God's love answers all questions and challenges [and] there is no limit to angels' healing power." All we have to do is ask for their help.[8]

Nick Bunick, author of *In God's Truth,* claims to have relived the apostle Paul's life through hypnotic regression, and he uses those memories to denounce what he calls inaccuracies and outright falsehoods in the New Testament. Bunick also expounds how inspirational messages of love are carried to earth by angelic beings.[9]

To some New Agers, angels are not only here to serve us, but they are proof of immortality. Death is seen only as a sort of energy transformation. James Redfield uses this premise in his best-selling book *The Celestine Prophecy.* Originally self-published in 1992, it grew from popularity only in New Age bookstores to an $850,000 purchase by Time Warner books, with sales rapidly surpassing a million copies. Redfield assures the reader that what we imagine as death is actually a smooth transition to a higher spiritual plane. *The Celestine Prophecy* states that as humans evolve, vibrating at higher levels, we become invisible to the less evolved among us. As distilled spiritual energy, we achieve virtual immortality. The future humankind, Redfield claims, will evolve into a spiritually enlightened culture of peace and harmony. Angels, like "the enlightened" in this case, are only visible to the "spiritually elite."

The Celestine Prophecy also claims: "When you have acquired enough energy, you are ready to consciously engage evolution . . . to produce the coincidences that will lead you forward." For people who have an extrabiblical view of angels, *The Celestine Prophecy* doesn't seem that difficult to believe; some angel books make similar assertions. According to Sophy Burnham, author of best-sellers *A Book of Angels* and *Angel Letters,* angels and other supernatural beings are constantly intervening in our lives. "People are looking for hope," says Burnham, who studied Buddhism and Hinduism. "In the media, we hear of so much horror and despair. But angels make us know we are loved—these wonderful beings are protecting us."[10]

So popular are these "spiritual" books that *The Celestine Prophecy* has already passed its hundredth week on the *New York Times* best-seller list, while sales of *A Book of Angels* has reached about 750,000. Angel books altogether have sold millions of copies—as many as books about alien abductions.

Drawing on popular psychology, experts on angels, aliens, and life after death deal in what is called "feeling realities." John Mack, a psychiatrist, writes that he would take seriously a person's alien-abduction story if "what was being reported was felt to be real by the experiencer . . . and communicated sincerely." These personal-development experts assert, the truth lies in what you feel, not what you "know in your head," much less what you can prove.[11]

Alma Daniel, the coauthor of *Ask Your Angels,* which has sold half a million copies in five languages, says an angel visit feels like this: "Angels come as unrestrained feelings and emotions. You may feel a sense of comfort, peace, security and joy for no reason. Rarely do they come in full regalia with wings and a harp. Sometimes they come as beloved pets . . . or a lovely odor with no apparent source."[12] Other angel greeters describe the experience as "warmth," "a tickle," "an embrace," "strength," "tingling," "an inner knowing," and "light."

These so-called angel experts suggest there are exceptions to reliance on feelings as evidence of truth. If, for instance, your feelings lead to disbelief instead of belief, then the feelings could be dismissed as some form of denial. According to them, there may be emotional as well as intellectual barriers to belief. For example, they consider that an unwillingness to believe in angels reflects a person's low self-esteem. *The Celestine Prophecy* can confidently demand that readers suspend their disbelief because it tells so many people precisely what they want to hear. *The Celestine Prophecy* workbook, a guide to the book, begins by stating, "Those who take a strictly intellectual approach to this subject will be the last to 'get it.' To change the world we must 'break through the habits of skepticism and denial.'"[13]

There are numerous Web sites dedicated to angels. Some speak from a faithfully biblical point of view while others deal with more arcane themes. One site I found while doing research for this book gave tips on how to communicate with your angel. The site explained that every time you hear that little voice inside your head that is usually called a conscience, it's actually your angel. Thinking loving thoughts and about loving actions—that is a message from your angel. Your guardian would never send you a message involving fear or negativity. The site encouraged readers to ask their angel for things. You may not always get exactly what you want, the site says, but it never hurts to ask.

I was shocked recently when a pastor friend from Norman, Oklahoma, showed me a book that a church member passed along to him. The book described various conversations the author has had over the years with his angel. The author has quizzed his angel many times about what it was like to be with Jesus, what heaven was like, and about the angel's presence at many events in church history. According to his credentials listed on the back of the book, the author has been a pastor for several years and was formerly an associate pastor at a well-known evangelical church in Tulsa, Oklahoma.

God's love compels us to share the whole truth of the gospel with the hurting, lost, sick, and broken. New Age "feel-good affirmations" can't heal the separation that sin has made between them and God. The lost don't need the self-satisfying counterfeits that are steeped in demonic deception. They need the truth that sets men free. Unfortunately, today's modern culture has turned the truth of God's Word upside down. Modern belief systems demand very little of their adherents. They preach that a good attitude is a substitute for good works. In a world where there is no sin, good works are not a requirement either. Instead of working out your salvation with fear and trembling, you can simply wait for an angelic visitation. This elevation of one's experience and feelings—over logic and God's Word—creates an angelology that appears to be made more from human (if not demonic) imagination than Divine devices.

Jesus gave his own blood on a cross to forgive sinners and make them whole. He came that we might enjoy life and live abundantly, not just "feel good about ourselves." Forgiveness is necessary because sin is a reality. There has always been a price for sin, but Jesus paid that price. Even now if we desire to be his, there is a price. Jesus said, "And you will be hated by all on account of My name, but it is the one who has endured to the end who will be saved" (Matt. 10:22).

As believers, we are open to deception when we believe God deals with us only at an emotional level. Some may believe we must "feel" God, and therefore they often resist receiving wise counsel. The reality is, God works in and through us despite our emotions. How you feel when you wake up in the morning does not change God. Your highest high and your lowest low may contradict the reality of any given situation. God has often blessed me when I was at my emotional worst. I could wake up on the wrong side of the bed, stumble over the cat, burn my breakfast, get a ticket on the way to work, arrive two hours late, and suddenly remember I have a three-hour dental appointment. None of that changes God's plan for my life or how he may use me that day.

As greater deception permeates the world, challenging the church at every turn, all believers will be faced with a choice: Be conformed to the world or be transformed by the renewing of our minds (see Rom. 12:2). Those who would rather die than compromise will find a joy unspeakable that the world cannot even imagine.

In some ways, it almost sounds disrespectful, if not downright irreverent, to not believe the story of the vanishing hitchhiker. Some say the story teaches people to be prepared for the Second Coming of Christ. Others say that whether it's true or not, it has quickened a renewed interest in God to those who hear it for the first time. The Bible truly does tell us we could entertain angels and not even be aware of it. With so much talk of angelic visitations, we all would like to think it could happen anywhere, at any time, and especially to us. But I'm afraid that the story of the vanishing hitchhiker is only a legend given wing by the power of a friend-of-a-friend's testimony.

CHAPTER FIVE

Busting Hell
Wide Open

➤ ◄

D id Russian scientists actually discover the gates of hell deep
inside the earth's core, or is the story of the "well to hell"
someone's idea of a practical joke?

The basis of this legend goes back to an actual *Scientific
American* article published in 1984 about an experimental well in
Russia's Kola Peninsula. The well reached a depth of 12 kilome-
ters into the ground where scientists encountered rare rock for-
mations, flows of gas and water, and incredibly high temperatures. From this article an urban legend was created, and the

genuine report on the digging somehow became embellished into a story of scientists discovering the earth's center and the sound of tormented screams.

I first read this larger-than-life story in a 1989 newsletter from a Christian television network. The front-page article said their account of Russian scientists discovering hell in the Kola Peninsula came from the translation of an article in a Finnish newspaper named *Ammennusatia*.

Author and talk-show host Rich Buhler discovered a reprint of the article and shares these details from the "Ship of Fools" Web site. The article reads in part:

> A geological group who drilled a hole about 14.4 kilometers deep in the crust of the earth are saying that they heard human screams. Screams have been heard from the condemned souls from earth's deepest hole. Terrified scientists are afraid they have let loose the evil powers of hell up to the earth's surface.
>
> "The information we are gathering is so surprising, that we are sincerely afraid of what we might find down there," stated Dr Azzacov, the manager of the project in remote Siberia.
>
> The second surprise was the high temperature they discovered in the earth's center. "The calculations indicate the given temperature was about 1,100 degrees Celsius, or over 2,000 degrees Fahrenheit," Azzacov pointed out. "This is far more then we expected. It seems almost like an inferno of fire is brutally going on in the center of the earth.
>
> "The last discovery was nevertheless the most shocking to our ears, so much so that the scientists are afraid to continue the project. We tried to listen to the earth's movements at certain intervals

with supersensitive microphones, which were let down through the hole. What we heard turned those logically thinking scientists into trembling ruins. It was sometimes a weak, but high pitched sound which we thought to be coming from our own equipment," explained Dr Azzacov.

"But after some adjustments we comprehended that indeed the sound came from the earth's interior. We could hardly believe our own ears. We heard a human voice, screaming in pain. Even though one voice was discernible, we could hear thousands, perhaps millions, in the background, of suffering souls screaming. After this ghastly discovery, about half of the scientists quit because of fear. Hopefully, that which is down there will stay there," Dr Azzacov added.[1]

According to the network's newsletter, a Texas evangelist who was a frequent guest on the network had given the Finnish article to them. So Buhler set out to track down the origin of this "well to hell" story. A call to the evangelist's office revealed the article came from a "respected scientific journal" in Finland. The evangelist's office said they had a letter from a Norwegian man, Age Rendalen, who had confirmed the story was indeed true. Regrettably, this is where the tale goes sour, for it turns out that Rendalen was a first-class prankster.

Mr. Rendalen was visiting California when he heard a broadcast saying that a well to the center of the earth had been dug and screams of torment and anguish had been heard. So Rendalen took the story back to Norway and mailed an account of it to a Christian magazine in Finland. A reader of Rendalen's account of the story then passed it on in the form of a letter to a Finnish missionary's newsletter. From there it returned to the United States, reaching both the Christian network and other evangelists who then claimed they had gotten it from a respected Finnish scientific journal.

Rendalen later sent a letter with a "translation" of the Finnish newspaper article, telling the network that he had visited the United States a few weeks earlier and happened upon their telecast about the "well to hell" story. In the letter he said: "I must confess that I laughed when I heard your account . . . . I did not believe one word of it, and commented to my friend that Americans sure were gullible to believe that hell could be physically located to a hole in the ground. I cannot even begin to tell you what a shock it was to me when I returned to Norway and found the newspapers full of reports about this incident. I knew immediately that if there was a hell, I for sure would end up in it. A tremendous fear took hold of me, and for two nights I dreamed about fire and screams until I surrendered to God and committed my life to his hands for safe-keeping."[2]

Rendalen encouraged the network not to let "skeptics" interfere with their telling of the story.

Rich Buhler's research paid off as he finally reached Rendalen at his home near Oslo. Age Rendalen quickly confessed to having fabricated every word of the story. He told Buhler that when he had visited the U.S. a few weeks earlier and had seen the host of a Christian television program enthusiastically relating the Drilling to Hell story, "I couldn't believe that the hosts really thought the story was true and that they would broadcast it without apparently having checked it out."[3]

This "well to hell" hoax and the subsequent phony letter sent to the Christian network by Rendalen could have easily been verified with a few simple calls. Unfortunately, this Christian urban legend has been reproduced in sermons, newsletters, tapes, and e-mails. Next to the Madalyn Murray O'Hair petition, this may be the single biggest hoax pulled on American believers.

The Book of 1 John, chapter 4, begins with a command to test what we hear: "Beloved, do not believe every spirit, but test the spirits to see whether they are from God; because many false prophets have gone out into the world."

A believer's tendency is to trust someone because they invoke the name of God, or to see a book in a Christian bookstore and assume it must be OK. John, however, urges us to not believe every spirit. He says that in order to learn the difference in truth and error, we need to start testing: "But try the spirits whether they are of God" (KJV). The word *try* here is present tense. It means to keep on trying. The reason is simple: "Many false prophets are gone out into the world" (KJV).

There are two motivating spirits at work in the world today: God's Spirit of Truth, who speaks through the inspired Word; and Satan's spirit of error, which teaches lies. "But the Spirit explicitly says that in later times some will fall away from the faith, paying attention to deceitful spirits and doctrines of demons" (1 Tim. 4:1).

God's representatives will speak the truth, and God's children will recognize them. Satan's workers will speak from, and depend on, worldly wisdom (1 Cor. 1:7–2:16). The true sheep recognize the voice of the Shepherd (John 10:1–5, 27–28). True sheep also recognize and love one another. Satan is a divider and destroyer; Christ unites people in love.

The apostle Paul warned the Ephesians about false prophets: "For I know this, that after my departing shall grievous wolves enter in among you, not sparing the flock. Also of your own selves shall men arise, speaking perverse things, to draw away disciples after them" (Acts 20:29–30 KJV).

These false doctrines come from deceivers who are only out for personal gain. Jesus said, "Beware of false prophets, which come to you in sheep's clothing, but inwardly they are ravening wolves" (Matt. 7:15 KJV). Again he warned his followers, "And many false prophets shall rise, and shall deceive many" (Matt. 24:11 KJV).

Satan is the master deceiver. He knows he can never take us from God, so instead he tries to destroy our trustworthiness and integrity. We've all been deceived to some degree at various times in our lives. Even now we may be walking in deception and not know it. But our goal should be to know the truth, speak the truth, and allow the truth to make people free.

This tale proves that no one is immune to the deceptiveness of repeating and spreading Christian urban legends. The story of the well to hell only goes to show the power of the media in breathing new life into dead bones.

CHAPTER SIX

The Missing Day

> ← →

Ever since Darwin came out with his erroneous theory of evolution, many Christians have been uncomfortable resolving the argument between science and religion. Many of us have the feeling deep down inside that science is trying to do away with the need for God. It hasn't always been this way. Years ago, Christians could justly claim to be leaders in most intellectual arenas. Similarly, science was once widely acknowledged to have its roots in a Christian perspective on nature. But modernism and humanism have elevated man's "wisdom" over and above God's wisdom, and mankind has made a god of his own intellectual prowess.

THE COST OF DECEPTION ←

Christians feel vindicated when scientific discoveries substantiate the truthfulness and inspiration of biblical events. For example, when doctors recently agreed that laughter could actually aid in promoting the healing process, Christians smiled, knowing all along that "a merry heart doeth good like a medicine" (Prov. 17:22 KJV).

So it was no surprise to some when word got out that our space program had verified an Old Testament story of the sun standing still. This story of science agreeing with the Bible has been promoted in sermons, church bulletins, and religious publications as factual and true. Now with the aid of the Internet, the urban legend of Joshua's missing day is spreading once again.

Here is a copy of the story that is being circulated in Christian circles:

> For all the scientists out there and for all the students who have a hard time convincing these people regarding the truth of the Bible, here's something that shows God's awesome creation and shows that He is still in control.
>
> Did you know that the space program is busy proving that what has been called "myth" in the Bible is true? Mr. Harold Hill, president of the Curtis Engine Company in Baltimore, Maryland, and a consultant in the space program, relates the following development.
>
> "I think one of the most amazing things that God has for us today happened recently to our astronauts and space scientists at Green Belt, Maryland. They were checking the position of the sun, moon, and planets out in space where they would be 100 years and 1000 years from now. We have to know this so we won't send a satellite up and have it bump into something later on in its orbits. We have to lay out the orbits in terms of

the life of the satellite, and where the planets will be so the whole thing will not bog down.

"They ran the computer measurement back and forth over the centuries and it came to a halt. The computer stopped and put up a red signal, which meant that there was something wrong either with the information fed into it or with the results as compared to the standards. They called in the service department to check it out and they said, 'What's wrong?' Well, they found there is a day missing in space in elapsed time. They scratched their heads and tore their hair. There was no answer.

"Finally, a Christian man on the team said, 'You know, one time I was in Sunday school and they talked about the sun standing still.' While they didn't believe him, they didn't have an answer either, so they said, 'Show us.' He got a Bible and went back to the book of Joshua where they found a pretty ridiculous statement for any one with 'common sense.'

"There they found the Lord saying to Joshua, 'Fear them not, I have delivered them into thy hand; there shall not a man of them stand before thee' (Josh. 10:8). Joshua was concerned because he was surrounded by the enemy and if darkness fell they would overpower them. So Joshua asked the Lord to make the sun stand still! That's right—'The sun stood still and the moon stayed—and hasted not to go down about a whole day!' (Josh. 10:13).

"The astronauts and scientists said, 'There is the missing day!' They checked the computers going back into the time it was written and found it was close but not close enough. The elapsed time that was missing back in Joshua's day was 23 hours and 20 minutes–not a whole day.

"They read the Bible and there it was 'about (approximately) a day' These little words in the Bible are important, but they were still in trouble because if you cannot account for 40 minutes you'll still be in trouble 1,000 years from now. Forty minutes had to be found because it can be multiplied many times over in orbits.

"As the Christian employee thought about it, he remembered somewhere in the Bible where it said the sun went backwards. The scientists told him he was out of his mind, but they got out the Book and read these words in Second Kings that told of the following story: Hezekiah, on his deathbed, was visited by the prophet Isaiah who told him that he was not going to die.

"Hezekiah asked for a sign as proof. Isaiah said 'Do you want the sun to go ahead 10 degrees?' Hezekiah said. 'It is nothing for the sun to go ahead 10 degrees, but let the shadow return backward 10 degrees.' Isaiah spoke to the Lord and the Lord brought the shadow 10 degrees backward!

"Ten degrees is exactly 40 minutes! Twenty-three hours and 20 minutes in Joshua, plus 40 minutes in Second Kings make the missing day in the universe!" Isn't it amazing?

References: Joshua 10:8 and 12–13 and 2 Kings 20:9–11.

The origin of Joshua's missing day goes back more than half a century. In his 1936 book *The Harmony of Science and Scripture,* Harry Rimmer devoted the entire last chapter to "Modern Science and the Long Day of Joshua." After recounting the story in Joshua, chapter 10, of how God made the sun stand still, Rimmer makes this observation: "The final testimony of science is that such a day left its record for all time. As long as time shall be, the record of this day must remain. The fact is attested by eminent men of science, two of whom I quote here."[1]

These two men turn out to be Sir Edwin Ball, a British astronomer, and Charles A. L. Totten, a Yale professor. Rimmer credits Ball with being the first to notice "twenty-four hours had been lost out of solar time." Rimmer also freely quotes from the work of Professor C. A. Totten of Yale, who wrote of Joshua's long day in his 1890 book *Joshua's Long Day and the Dial of Ahaz*. Totten, an instructor who taught military science and tactics at Yale from 1889 to 1892, was known to also have preached anti-Semitism and several times predicted the coming Apocalypse. In the final chapter of his book, Rimmer offers a summary of Totten's work in which he says he can prove exactly how the lost day had been discovered. Using biblical numerology and his own calculations, Totten even gave the exact day and month on which Joshua's battle was fought—Tuesday, July 22.

When Dr. Rimmer's book was first published, it apparently caused a bit of a stir, and was accepted by those anxious to show how science "proved" the Bible to be true. The story sat mostly forgotten until the 1960s, when the space race was causing great excitement about the exploration of our universe. Each space shot brought new discoveries but also gave man more of a sense of being in control of his universe. This new knowledge quickly widened the gap between science and religion. So it was no wonder that Christians were elated when the story of Joshua's missing day circulated once again.

The story of Joshua's missing day became news again in 1969 when columnist Mary Kathryn Bryan, writing for *The Spencer Evening World* in Spencer, Indiana, reported on one of Harold Hill's speaking engagements where Hill told the story about NASA's discovery of the missing day in time.

The paper started receiving requests from all over the world for reprints of the article. From there the Missing Day story found its way into untold numbers of magazines, newspapers, gospel tracts, and books. Harold Hill himself included the account in his 1974 book *How to Live Like a King's Kid*. In the last chapter of the book, Hill states that on occasion he spoke to high school and college students regarding Bible and science topics. When the subject turned to his involvement in the space program at Goddard, Hill told students, "I was involved from the start, through contractual arrangements with my company."[2]

Actually, it turned out Hill wasn't a consultant in the space program as was previously claimed. He was president of the Curtis Engine Company, a company that had a contract with NASA to service electrical generators, but he never was connected in any way with the planning of mission operations.

In his book Hill also acknowledged that he did not personally witness the incident at NASA, and said that he could not remember where he first heard the story, but insisted that "my inability to furnish documentation of the 'Missing day' incident in no way detracts from its authenticity."

Hill also said, "Later, someone sent me a clipping . . . saying I had admitted the whole thing was a hoax. Shortly thereafter, numerous religious magazines, some of them Christian, began repeating the false 'retraction' and apologizing for their original participation in the rerun of the article. Not one of them ever checked with me as to the truth or error of the article as originally published. For the record—the report is true, the retraction false. . . . The whole sequence of events has demonstrated to me how prone even Christians are to believe a lie instead of the truth."[3]

In a July 1989 "Bible-Science Newsletter" article, Paul Bartz reports about the discrepancies in Hill's story: "Dr. Bolton Davidheiser wrote the NASA office at Greenbelt, Maryland, where all of this was supposed to have happened. They replied that they knew nothing of Mr. Harold Hill and could not corroborate the 'lost day' reference. . . . The concluding paragraph of NASA's letter read, 'Although we make use of planetary positions as necessary in the determination of spacecraft orbits on our computers, I have not found that any "astronauts and space scientists at Greenbelt" were involved in the "lost day" story attributed to Mr. Hill.'"[4]

A Baptist minister from North Carolina wrote a letter to the "Urban Legends Research Centre" Web site concerning the legend of the missing day. In part he said:

> Do I think some Christians might believe a tale like "NASA finds the lost day in time"? You bet your boots I do!
>
> Some people need to find objective and empirical proof for their spiritual and religious beliefs. It gives them a sense of security to find something that proves and supports their faith.
>
> In the past, things that could not be explained or understood were attributed to God. As science explains more, there are less things that are mysterious. This is threatening to the faith of some people. For some people, the affirmation of a miracle in the Bible by scientists is the ultimate proof (to them) that their faith is valid. This "Lost Day" hoax would be a powerful attraction to these people.
>
> Sometimes these people get very emotional in defending their beliefs. Many times their reaction is to take a closed-minded stand. "The Bible says it, I believe it and that settles it." (i.e. "don't confuse me with the facts.")[5]

As Christians we understand the importance of truth. Therefore we should do all we can to avoid the dissemination of erroneous material, regardless of how good the evidence may appear. Attempting to defend God's Word with myths and hoaxes will ultimately do the body of Christ more harm. As believers we often feel threatened trying to separate "fact" from "faith." It seems as if we can't reconcile the use of both science and the Bible. For example, very few believers could successfully argue their beliefs in a debate of creation versus evolution and would be very intimidated if called upon to do so. We should always be ready to give a good reply when asked to defend what we believe. A little bit of common sense and a small amount of research can make us ready to have an apt answer when called upon. "For the time will come when they will not endure sound doctrine; but *wanting* to have their ears tickled, they will accumulate for themselves teachers in accordance to their own desires; and will turn away their ears from the truth, and will turn aside to myths" (2 Tim. 4:3–4, italics added).

With so much at stake and our beliefs being challenged by those who want scientific proof for our claims, now is the time to sharpen our devotion to the Word.

Many in the world have sought to make a god of science and empirical reasoning. Faith is of no use to them. These false idols have always been in this world, but the danger to us is when we allow ourselves to be misled by myths. Because we often won't take the time to investigate stories any further before repeating them, these legends become legitimized by what we believe are credible sources and reliable facts. We must be slow to speak and quick to listen because the origin of a story is not as important as how it circulates.

Unfortunately, there are some in the church who have joined forces with the humanistic philosophers and psychologists, the evolutionists, and other so-called teachers admittedly bereft of God. But God is raising up a generation of people who, like Daniel's friends, will not bow to the idols when the music plays, who will stand in the midst of ridicule and persecution. These will become leaders who persevere, point out the errors of our ways, and give us much needed direction.

CHAPTER SEVEN

As Seen on TV
↭ ↫

Procter & Gamble is one of the oldest and most respected companies in the United States. They manufacture a variety of quality products for the home, such as soap, food, coffee, shampoo, and cold remedies. They are the sponsors of many of the daytime soap operas, and chances are you have used their products.

So I was skeptical when I first heard that the president of Procter & Gamble appeared on a recent talk show to admit his company's ties to the satanic church. It didn't make any sense that an executive would go on national television to announce something so explosive and potentially damaging to his company. This story turned out to be another Christian urban legend.

A petition was quickly made and photocopied that maintained the Procter & Gamble moon and stars trademark is the sign of the Church of Satan and was put on the company's products by the company's president at the request of the church. Christians were encouraged to boycott Procter & Gamble products as a way of proving to the president that "there are more than enough Christians and others who believe in God to put a very large dent into his profits." A list of the company's products was quickly readied and made available by several ministries and church organizations. This is a part of the protest letter and petition I received in May 1998:

PLEASE MAKE A DIFFERENCE

The President of Procter & Gamble appeared on the Phil Donahue Show on March 1, 1994. He announced that due to the openness of our society, he was coming out of the closet about his association with the church of Satan. He stated that a large portion of his profits from Procter & Gamble Products goes to support this satanic church. When asked by Donahue if stating this on TV would hurt his business, he replied, "There are not enough Christians in the United States to make a difference."

If you are not sure about the product, look for "Procter & Gamble" written on the products, or the symbol of a ram's horn, which will appear on each product beginning in April. The ram's horn will form the 666, which is known as Satan's number. Christians should remember that if they purchase any of these products, they will be contributing to the Church of Satan. Inform other

Christians about this and STOP buying Procter &
Gamble products. Let's show Procter & Gamble
that there are enough Christians to make a difference. On a previous Merv Griffin Show, the
owner of Procter & Gamble said that if Satan
would prosper he would give his heart and soul to
him. Then he gave Satan credit for his riches.

We urge you to make copies of this and pass it
on to as many people as possible. This needs to
stop. Liz Claiborne also professes to worship Satan
and recently openly admitted on the Oprah
Winfrey show that half of her profits go towards
the Church of Satan.

Ironically, no one seems to be able to decide which talk show
the Procter & Gamble president actually appeared on. *Donahue*
was the most popular talk show at that time, but some versions of
the legend say that the appearance was actually on *The Merv
Griffin Show, Sally Jesse Raphael, The Oprah Winfrey Show,* or even
more recently, *Larry King Live*.

Amazingly, since this legend came to life in the early nineties
no one has ever produced a video or audiotape, or so much as a
transcript of the show where this allegedly happened. No one has
ever been able to confirm an airdate, time, or the exact program
on which the appearance took place, and no one seems to be able
to even name the person from Procter & Gamble who purport-
edly did the interview. Of course, Procter & Gamble has denied
any such appearance by anyone associated with the company, and
that their logo has ever had any satanic meaning. As a result of
this legend, Procter & Gamble stopped using the traditional logo
and designed a new one for its products.

Over the years, Procter & Gamble has answered more than
150,000 calls and letters about this legend and is still getting as
many as 80 calls a month as of this writing. Regardless, there are
some Christian Web sites that continue to promote the boycott.

To help put an end to this false report, the company requested major religious leaders from all backgrounds of faith to issue statements of support. Copies of these letters can be seen on Web sites from such well-known ministries as the Billy Graham Evangelistic Association, the Southern Baptist Convention, Jerry Falwell, and the Archbishop of Cincinnati. Even the Procter & Gamble home Web page has letters posted from talk show producers, other religious leaders, and the current company president all debunking this myth. The company is desperately trying to spread the word to the Christian community that there simply is no truth to the rumor.

So how did this Christian urban legend originate? According to Gary Alan Fine, a Georgia sociology professor and author of a book on contemporary legends, "Many Americans have long mistrusted large companies, whose inner workings are mysterious to them." Bill Ellis, associate professor of American Studies at Penn State University at Hazleton adds: "There's an implicit belief that for anyone to become really economically powerful, there must be some implicit deal with the forces of evil."[1]

So what is the truth about the moon and stars logo? In the nineteenth century, Procter & Gamble was more famous for its candles than its soap, which they shipped down the Ohio and Mississippi Rivers from Cincinnati to New Orleans. All the shipping crates were built by hand at the loading docks in Cincinnati. There the crate builders marked each crate by carving or burning their own individual logo into the wood. Procter & Gamble allowed the crate-makers to mark their crates, but wanted them to choose just one symbol. So a contest was held, and the man-in-the-moon-with-stars symbol created by one worker was chosen as the winner. That became the traditional trademark symbol of the company for many years.

MCDONALD'S

In another bedeviled executive legend, former McDonald's chairman, the late Ray Kroc, supposedly appeared on a talk show in 1977, admitting to Satanism and bragging about the financial support McDonald's supplied to the Church of Satan. In some towns, customers boycotted the golden arches, and children even quit their McDonald's-sponsored Little League teams.

LIZ CLAIBORNE

In another legend similar to the Procter & Gamble myth, designer Liz Claiborne supposedly appeared on *The Oprah Winfrey Show,* claiming that she was a devil worshiper, her company logo was a satanic symbol, and that she donated some of her profits to a satanic organization. As the story goes, Oprah, who had been wearing a Liz Claiborne dress, left the studio, and returned wearing a bathrobe, saying, "I'm never wearing one of your dresses again." According to the rumor traced back to 1990, Claiborne appeared as a guest on *The Oprah Winfrey Show* and said her company gave 30 percent of its profits to the Church of Satan. One version adds the eerie twist that as Claiborne was making her announcement, the television picture unexpectedly faded out, and when the picture came back, she wasn't there.

Another hoax has Claiborne stating her "reasons" for not wanting to design for black women. She is quoted as saying she doesn't need their money and they make her clothes look awful. The truth is Liz Claiborne retired from the company in 1989, two years before she allegedly made the comment about "designing for black women" and a year before the "I'm a Satanist" confession. Claiborne has also never appeared on Oprah Winfrey's talk show and no record of racist comments can be attributed to her.

TOMMY HILFIGER

Another version of the "racist designer" hoax came into being in 1995, this time involving Tommy Hilfiger. Allegedly he had appeared on any number of talk shows making this careless comment, "If I knew Blacks and Asians were going to wear my clothes, I would have never designed them." This prompted a boycott of his clothing line among those hoodwinked by the hoax. In an attempt to diffuse the urban legend, this announcement appears on the official Web page for Tommy Hilfiger: "For nearly two years now, an ugly rumor has been circulating about our company. Since you still may be the recipient of false information, we wanted to set the record straight and update you on important information. The facts remain simple and cannot be disputed. Tommy Hilfiger did not make the alleged inappropriate racial comments. He has never appeared on *The Oprah Winfrey Show,* although the rumor specifically asserts that he made negative remarks in that forum and that Ms. Winfrey asked him to leave. In fact, Ms. Winfrey herself, on her January 11, 1999, program, stated Tommy Hilfiger has never been on her show nor has she ever met him."[2]

JANET RENO ON THE "CHRISTIAN THREAT"

Politicians are used to having their every word scrutinized. Many times their words are taken out of context, and often they suffer the symptoms of foot-in-mouth disease. Former U.S. Attorney General Janet Reno takes the brunt of this legend that allegedly occurred on a national news program. Supposedly, in a 1994 interview with CBS's *60 Minutes,* Reno was asked to define a cultist. According to the account, she is quoted as saying: "A cultist is one who has a strong belief in the Bible and the Second Coming of Christ; who frequently attends Bible studies; who has a high level of financial giving to a Christian cause; who home schools for their children; who has accumulated survival foods and has a strong belief in the Second Amendment; and who distrusts big government. Any of these may qualify but certainly more than one would cause us to look at this person as a threat, and his family as being in a risk situation that qualified for government interference."

If we believe this statement, the U.S. Attorney General's definition of a "cultist" would include any Christian or anyone mistrustful of government. The reality is Janet Reno was not interviewed by *60 Minutes* at any time during 1994, nor did she ever make such a statement. Like the other myths mentioned so far, no one can find any recording or transcript she ever made any such statement. An e-mail message has been circulating for some time now, alerting Christians to Reno's intimidating remarks. Usually these messages end with the following comments: "Do you qualify?? Are you a threat? This worries me. Does it worry you? Everyone in this country, 'the land of the free,' with computer access should copy this and send to every other man, woman and child who can read."

What does worry me is that most believers don't take enough time to verify "facts" before becoming participants in the propagation of legends that ultimately make us all look foolish.

WARNING TO THE RUMOR MILL

Scripture cautions us several times about the dangers of misjudging fabricated reports. These legends do nothing but motivate Christians to take up arms against rumor targets, ultimately wasting time and energy. Paul warned the church at Colossae: "See to it that no one takes you captive through philosophy and empty deception, according to the tradition of men, according to the elementary principles of the world, rather than according to Christ" (Col. 2:8).

His advice to Timothy is valid for us today: "Timothy, guard what has been entrusted to you, avoiding worldly and empty chatter and the opposing arguments of what is falsely called 'knowledge'" (1 Tim. 6:20).

In 1996, my dear mother died of pancreatic cancer. It wasn't detected until June that year, and by October she was gone. Friends in the medical field have told me that pancreatic cancer is very difficult to detect. Once it is discovered though, a patient has, at best, a few months to live. Like the subtle growth of this cancer, deception often works slowly and imperceptibly. Its influence grows and spreads until the victim is totally unaware he has ingested sufficient poisonous belief to do great harm. "And Jesus said to them, 'Watch out and beware of the leaven of the Pharisees and Sadducees'" (Matt. 16:6).

"Then they understood that He did not say to beware of the leaven of bread, but of the teaching of the Pharisees and Sadducees" (Matt. 16:12).

The very nature of deception is that those completely in its grasp are not able to comprehend the depth of their deception until God reveals it. To sit at the feet of false teachers is to become as they are, polluted and stained and full of dead men's bones. To stay in this contaminated state can result in significant doctrinal error and moral compromise. We must daily seek Christ as our wisdom and ask for discernment in how to walk with God.

CHAPTER EIGHT

Be Afraid, Be Very Afraid

→ ←

For years rumors have been circulating that HIV-infected needles are being left in places such as movie theater seats, pay phone coin return slots, and even pay phone earpieces. The movie theater pinprick story is just the latest version of an urban legend that has been around since the 1930s. Back then the legend was about a nefarious figure known as the Needle Man.

I remember hearing my older sisters warn me as a boy growing up in the sixties about the Needle Man. This evil individual, or in some versions, a group of men, allegedly left needles filled with morphine in theatre seats in hopes of kidnapping children and selling them as slaves.

Interestingly, as early as 1998, warnings about infected needles have been posted on Internet sites and forwarded to thousands by e-mail. Here is a copy of one such warning a friend of mine received in December 1999.

Warning—must read!

Be careful the next time you go to a cinema. These people could be anywhere!! An experience of a friend of my brother's wife left me speechless. Please do send this out to everyone you know. This incident occurred in Bombay's Metro cinema (among the best in town).

There was a group of 6-7 college girls & they went to the theater to see a movie. During the show one of the girls felt a slight pinprick but did not pay much attention to it. After some time that place began to itch. So she scratched herself and then saw a bit of blood on her hands. She assumed that she had caused it. At the end of the show, her friend noticed a sticker on her dress and read the caption. It read "Welcome to the world of AIDS." She tried to pass it off as a practical joke, but when she went for a blood test a couple of weeks later (just to be sure), she found herself HIV-positive.

When she complained to the cops, they mentioned that her story was one of many such cases they had received. It seems the operator uses a syringe to transfer a bit of his/her infected blood to the person sitting ahead of him/her. A horrible experience for the victim as also the family & friends. The WORST bit is that the person who does it gains NOTHING where as the victim loses EVERYTHING.

So, be careful . . .

Like most urban legends, there are numerous variations to the story. Here is another version of the "pinprick" legend:

> Please check your chairs when going to the movie theatres!!!!
>
> An incident occurred when a friend's co-worker went to sit in a chair and something was poking her. She then got up and found that it was a needle with a little note at the end. It said, "Welcome to the real world, you're 'HIV POSI-TIVE.'"
>
> Doctors tested the needle and it was HIV POSITIVE. We don't know which theater this happened at, but it happened in Hawaii.
>
> "BE CAUTIOUS WHEN GOING TO THE MOVIES!!!!!!!!!"
>
> IF YOU MUST GO TO THE MOVIES, PLEASE, PLEASE CHECK!!!!! One of the safest ways is NOT sticking your hands between the seats, but moving the seat part way up and down a few times and REALLY LOOK!!!!!!! Most of us just plop down into the seats.

Though the possibility exists that needles can be left in theater seats or pay phone coin returns, it has been difficult to find actual evidence that this is happening on a frequent basis at any local theater. There has been only one legitimate report in 1996 of a man in Louisiana being stuck by a needle in a theater, but there has been no further information that he contracted any infection or disease. To this date, there are no known instances of contaminated needles turning up in pay phone coin returns, let alone an unsuspecting telephone user being infected by a needle in the phone's earpiece.

The Centers for Disease Control and Prevention (CDC), located in Atlanta, Georgia, has been inundated with requests for more information about this urban legend. Here is a copy of the CDC's response to the public's concern from their official Web site: "CDC has received inquiries about a variety of reports or warnings about used needles left by HIV-infected injection drug users in coin return slots of pay phones and movie theater seats. These reports and warnings are being circulated on the Internet and by e-mail and fax. Some reports have falsely indicated that CDC 'confirmed' the presence of HIV in the needles. CDC has not tested such needles nor has CDC confirmed the presence or absence of HIV in any sample related to these rumors. The majority of these reports and warnings appear to have no foundation in fact."[1]

The best advice for anyone who is injured from a needle stick is to immediately contact his or her physician or go to an emergency room. The injury should be reported to the local or state health departments.

SNAKES IN THE BALL PIT

Poisonous snakes can be found in several areas of the United States. Rattlesnakes for instance are indigenous to my home state, Oklahoma. What most people don't know is that rattlesnakes are mostly found in dry and rocky conditions, they aren't likely to be found in populous areas like your neighborhood or commercial areas. That fact alone, however, hasn't been enough to squelch the urban legend about venomous snakes lurking in the ball pits of some fast food restaurant's playgrounds. This e-mail warning might give the recipients reason to fear allowing little ones to play at the playground at Burger King. The message reads:

> You Should Know This.
> About a week or so ago, a mother took her

eager 3-year-old son to Burger King for lunch.
After they ate their lunch, the mother said that the
son could go and play on the playground for a
while since he ate all his lunch.

She watched as the boy played in the tunnels,
on the slide, and in the ball pit. The boy played
for about 10 minutes when he started to whimper
slightly.

The mother asked the boy what had happened
and he merely replied, "Hurt mommy." The
mother assumed that the little boy had banged his
elbow or something while playing.

They left to return home. A half an hour after
they were home, the mother noticed some big red
welts on the little boys arms and legs. Not being
able to figure out what they were, the mother
started to look at them closer. Could be red ant
bites . . . she did not know.

An hour later, the little boy died. Come to
find out, when returning to Burger King to see
if there were red ants in the play area, in case
the little boy had an allergic reaction, Burger
King employees and she discovered that there
was a family of baby rattlesnakes living under-
neath the balls in the ball-pit area. She has since
found out that this happens more frequently
than not. The snakes will crawl into the ball pit
because it is dark and warm in there. She knows
for a fact that another death has occurred
because of this in South Carolina. Please use
caution when letting any children play in an outside play area of a fast food restaurant, this
could happen anywhere. Burger Kings are now
building their play areas inside the buildings for
a safer environment.

HYPODERMICS AND HEROIN

Another variation involves Burger King's competitor McDonald's. This one appears valid to many as it gives more details, like the names of the mother and the child and the city in which this supposedly happened. This is a copy of the e-mail hoax:

> My name is Lauren Archer. My son Kevin and I lived in Midland, Texas. On October 2, 1999, I took my only son to McDonald's for his 3rd birthday. After he finished lunch, I allowed him to play in the ball pit. When he started whining later on, I asked him what was wrong, he pointed to the back of his pull-up's and simply said "Mommy, it hurts." But I couldn't find anything wrong with him at that time. I bathed him when we got home, and it was at that point when I found a welt on his left buttock. Upon investigating, it seemed as if there was something like a splinter under the welt. I made an appointment to have it taken out the next day, but soon he started vomiting and shaking, then his eyes rolled back into his head. From there, we went to the emergency room. He died later that night. It turned out that the welt on his buttock was the tip of a hypodermic needle that had broken off inside. The autopsy revealed that Kevin had died from a heroin overdose. The next week, the police removed the balls from the ball pit. There was rotten food, several hypodermic needles: some full; some used; knives, half-eaten candy, diapers, feces, and the stench of urine. If a child is not safe in a child's play area, then where? You can find the article on Kevin Archer in the October 10, 1999,

issue of the Midland Chronicle. Please forward
this to all loving mothers!

This would be a terrible tragedy if it were at all true. The real
newspaper in Midland, the *Midland Reporter-Telegram,* has no
record in its archives of a boy named Kevin Archer who died at a
Midland McDonald's.

There certainly may be a lot of lost items floating around in a
playground ball pit, such as food, shoes, gum, and candy, but
there probably are not venomous snakes lurking about. Neither
are there heroin-filled needles.

The Burger King Corporation has taken measures to assure
their patrons that their playground ball pits are not a breeding
ground for fear. A statement found on their corporate Web site in
part says this: "To be positively clear, the incident outlined in the
e-mail has no basis in fact relative to any Burger King® restau-
rants. Burger King Corporation takes the dissemination of this
false rumor very seriously and will vigorously pursue any and all
remedies available to us against the originator(s) to the fullest
extent allowed by law."[2]

BLUE STAR LSD

With drugs continuing to be a scourge in our society, this next
hoax has grabbed the attention of parents and teachers alike. You
may have seen a warning to parents posted in your local schools
about the "Blue Star LSD" tattoo. Since the eighties, police
departments and elementary schools have circulated this warning
using photocopied flyers. The flyers have been sent to numerous
schools, daycares, hospitals, and police stations warning that
LSD-laden, lick-and-stick tattoo transfers are being given to children in local schoolyards. These harmless looking tattoos, the size
of a pencil eraser, are on small pieces of paper containing a blue
star. Each star is believed to be soaked with LSD.

A typical flyer contains this information:

The drug is absorbed through the skin simply by HANDLING THE PAPER. There are also brightly colored paper tattoos resembling postage stamps that have the picture of one of the following:

Superman, Mickey Mouse, Clowns, Disney Characters, Bart Simpson or Butterflies

Each one is wrapped in foil. This is a new way of selling acid by appealing to young children. These are laced with DRUGS.

If your child gets any of the above, do not handle them. These are known to react quickly and some are laced with strychnine.

Symptoms: Hallucinations, severe vomiting, uncontrolled laughter, mood changes, change in body temperature.

Please feel free to reproduce this article and distribute it within your community and work place. Get the word out about this danger to our children.

From: J. O'Donnel—Danbury Hospital— Outpatient Chemical Dependency Treatment Service

Please copy and post it at your work, give to friends, send a copy to your local schools. This is very serious—young lives have already been taken.

This is growing faster than we can warn parents and professionals.

Dave Gross, who operates "The Blue Star LSD FAQ" (frequently asked questions) Web site, said that despite this legend's many variations these facts are typically always included in every version of the warning:

- These drugs are packaged in a red cardboard box wrapped in foil.

- Dealers or older children give these drugs to younger children either for kicks or to hook new customers.
- These drugs are known to react very quickly and some are laced with strychnine.
- These tattoos could cause a "fatal 'trip'" in children.
- Many children have already died from accidental ingestion of these tattoos.
- You should spread the word of this danger far and wide.[3]

Folklorist Jan Harold Brunvand wrote about rumors of "Mickey Mouse Acid" in his 1984 book *The Choking Doberman*. He called it "the most insidious urban drug legend" because it describes how LSD dealers try to make addicts of our young children by polluting the image of Mickey Mouse himself.[4]

Believing this flyer to be true, parents have earnestly handed out photocopies of the warning at PTA meetings, school functions, and throughout neighborhoods. Churches have not been immune from this hoax either. Dave Gross states that the church may have helped perpetuate the myth. "All it took from there was a church group copying the hazily-understood information into an anti-drug flyer and 'the legend was on a roll.'"[5]

Are children really in danger of getting dosed with LSD through drug-laced tattoos? So far there is no evidence to prove they are. Are believers in a position to cause unnecessary fear? In a word, yes. When it comes to drugs and forwarding this bogus warning to others, "just say no."

THE HEADLIGHT KILLERS

With all the alarm caused by gang violence in our major cities, the following two urban legends sound like they might be true. The first story tells about a "new gang initiation ritual" that has become prevalent in major cities in America. Gang members supposedly drive the highways and side streets at night with their headlights off. The first motorist who flashes their lights as a courtesy reminder to turn on their lights becomes the intended target. The gang members follow the unsuspecting Good

Samaritan and when the gang members pull alongside, the new initiate must gun down the driver without mercy.

The recent horror film *Urban Legend,* in which this "Lights Out" legend figured prominently, helped spark a flurry of panicked inquiries to police departments in localities all over the U.S. John Moore, senior research associate at the National Youth Gang Center, based in Tallahassee, confirmed for the *Washington Post* in November 1998 that the "Lights Out" story was false: "I know of no incident in the country where this type of thing occurred," he told the *Post.* "This is one of the wonders of the Internet, that you can take something that has no basis in fact and make people believe it."[6]

While maintaining that the story is fictitious, some law enforcement agencies recommend the public play it safe when driving in areas where gang activities take place. They fear that growing publicity could spark a copycat occurrence like that in the film.

"SPUNKBALL"

The other legend claims teenagers are playing a deadly game on the nation's roads by tossing firebombs into vehicle windows. Here, in part, is a duplicate of the infamous e-mail warning:

> I just wanted to warn all of my friends about something that has been occurring more and more lately, all throughout the country.
>
> Groups of teenagers have been caught, in alarming numbers, playing a new and dangerous game called Spunkball. Spunkball consists of a group of teens in a car pulling up to a stoplight and looking around for a car stopped nearby with an open window. When one is spotted, the teens shout, "Spunkball," and throw a gasoline-soaked rag that has been wrapped in aluminum foil through the open window.

Spunkball playing has already claimed two
lives, caused uncountable injuries due to burns,
and caused thousands of dollars in damage to
automobiles. The best defense, say authorities, is
to keep all windows rolled up when stopped at
traffic lights, as only cars with windows down are
being targeted.

If you are at a red light and hear a shout of
"Spunkball," and notice something come flying in
your window, the best thing to do is to have all
passengers immediately exit the vehicle. DO NOT
try to retrieve the object, as it will ignite once the
firecracker explodes.

PLEASE PASS THIS ON TO EVERYONE
YOU CARE ABOUT.

Reports like this only add to the fear in our society that perhaps there are new twists to the delinquency perpetrated by
young people. So far there have been no valid reports of
"Spunkball" ever happening in any city.

FLESH-EATING BANANAS

With growing concerns over pesticides and the chemicals used
on today's produce, it's easy to understand the concern consumers would have when they first heard this next legend on the
news. It seems the University of California-Riverside may accidentally be responsible for originating a hoax about bad bananas
from Costa Rica. In February 2000 I received from a friend this
e-mail warning:

Several shipments of bananas from Costa
Rica have been infected with necrotizing fasciitis, otherwise known as flesh-eating bacteria.
Recently this disease has decimated the monkey
population in Costa Rica. We are now just

learning that the disease has been able to graft itself to the skin of fruits in the region, most notably the banana, which is Costa Rica's largest export. Until this finding, scientists were not sure how the infection was being transmitted. It is advised not to purchase bananas for the next three weeks as this is the period of time for which bananas that have been shipped to the U.S. with the possibility of carrying this disease. If you have eaten a banana in the last 2-3 days and come down with a fever followed by a skin infection, seek medical attention! The skin infection from necrotizing fasciitis is very painful and eats two to three centimeters of flesh per hour. Amputation is likely, death is possible. . . . If you are more than an hour from a medical center, burning the flesh ahead of the infected area is advised to help slow the spread of the infection. The FDA has been reluctant to issue a countrywide warning because of fear of a nationwide panic. They have secretly admitted that they feel upwards of 15,000 Americans will be affected by this but that these are "acceptable numbers." Please forward this to as many of the people you care about as possible, as we do not feel 15,000 people is an acceptable number.

The Manheim Research Institute

Other variations of this hoax listed the Manheim Institute as working with the Centers for Disease Control and Prevention to warn consumers of the flesh-eating bacteria. The CDC denies this on their Web site: "The Centers for Disease Control and Prevention, National Center for Infectious Diseases, states that the current e-mail rumor circulating about Costa Rican bananas causing the disease 'necrotizing fasciitis' is false. We have not heard any reports of cases of necrotizing fasciitis associated with bananas. There is no evidence that necrotizing fasciitis is transmitted by food. The bacteria which most commonly cause necrotizing fasciitis live in the human body. The usual route of transmission for these bacteria is from person to person."[7]

Actual news reports have stated that an unnamed employee of the University of California-Riverside viewed this e-mail as a practical joke and passed it along to some friends outside the university. However, the staff member's computer automatically added her name along with the name of the university's office as a postscript to the e-mail. When the hoax began to circulate, it appeared to be an official memorandum from the University of California-Riverside.

THE "BLUSHING GLUTEUS" SPIDER

Now for my favorite legend currently making the cyberspace rounds. Read this one closely and see if you can spot the misinformation in this e-mail warning.

> According to an article by Dr. Beverly Clark in the Journal of the United Medical Association (JUMA), the mystery behind a recent spate of deaths has been solved.
>
> If you haven't already heard about it in the news, here is what happened. Three women in Chicago turned up at hospitals over a 5-day period, all with the same symptoms: fever, chills, and vomiting, followed by muscular collapse, paralysis, and finally, death. There were no outward signs of trauma. Autopsy results showed toxicity in the blood.
>
> These women did not know each other, and seemed to have nothing in common. It was discovered, however, that they had all visited the

same restaurant (Big Chappies at Blare Airport), within days of their deaths.

The health department descended on the restaurant, shutting it down. The food, water, and air conditioning were all inspected and tested, to no avail.

The big break came when a waitress at the restaurant was rushed to the hospital with similar symptoms. She told doctors that she had been on vacation, and had only gone to the restaurant to pick up her check. She did not eat or drink while she was there, but had used the rest room.

That is when one toxicologist, remembering an article he had read, drove out to the restaurant, went into the rest room, and lifted the toilet seat. Under the seat, out of normal view, was a small spider.

The spider was captured and brought back to the lab, where it was determined to be the South American Blush Spider (arachnius gluteus), so named because of its reddened flesh color. This spider's venom is extremely toxic, but can take several days to take effect. They live in cold, dark, damp, climates, and toilet rims provide just the right atmosphere.

Several days later a lawyer from Los Angeles showed up at a hospital emergency room. Before his death, he told the doctor that he had been away on business, had taken a flight from New York, changing planes in Chicago before returning home. He did not visit Big Chappies while there. He did, as did all of the other victims, have what was determined to be a puncture wound on his right buttock.

Investigators discovered that the flight he was on had originated in South America. The Civilian

Aeronautics Board (CAB) ordered an immediate inspection of the toilets of all flights from South America, and discovered the Blush spider's nests on 4 different planes!

It is now believed that these spiders can be anywhere in the country. So please, before you use a public toilet, lift the seat to check for spiders. It can save your life! And please pass this on to everyone you care about.

If you still need help seeing the flaws in this story, don't panic. It gives itself away in the first sentence: "According to an article by Dr. Beverly Clark in the Journal of the United Medical Association (JUMA). . . ." There is no "Journal of the United Medical Association." It's easy to confuse it with JAMA, the *Journal of the American Medical Association*. But still harder to confirm is the fact that there is no Dr. Beverly Clark in the imaginary journal, no news reports of spider-caused deaths among air travelers in Chicago, no Blare Airport in Chicago (it's O'Hare International Airport), and finally, there's no restaurant called "Big Chappies."

If this is not enough to expose this story as a hoax, just read the name of the spider again. It is the dreaded "arachnius gluteus." In Latin, *Arachnius* means spider and *gluteus* means, well, ah, let's just say it's the muscle you're sitting on.

THE CURE

We would never imagine that our friends or loved ones would purposefully deceive us with hoaxes and half-truths. Nor would we want to mislead those close to us. It may be that we view passing along the warnings of coming destruction, danger, or doom found in most urban legends as a means of deliverance, saving our loved ones from danger. Nevertheless, we may be unintentionally adding fuel to the fire when we repeat these stories without first checking out their validity.

Fear is a marvelous gift from God. Because of it we don't run into traffic or jump from tall buildings. To overcome our fears as children, we learn the safety of a mother's love or a father's embrace. But many times our fears are unwarranted or even irrational. I wonder what it is that keeps us bound up and immobilized with fear? What could we accomplish today if we moved in faith and reason?

Francis Bacon wrote, "Men fear death as children fear to go in the dark; and as that natural fear in children is increased with tales, so is the other."[8] Fear is the emotion that tells us that something is threatening our well being. It warns us of danger, that something isn't right for us—whether a physical danger or a threat to us emotionally. The threat can be real or imagined, and Christians are not immune to it. We too may tremble from ominous things or frightening news.

Fear can be a spiritual problem. Left to ourselves, we will never deal with it properly. All we will succeed in doing is masking and hiding what we fear. The only way to have victory over our fears is to allow God to separate us from what we feel is our strength, and to fear him instead. With a world watching, how we handle these boogie men may affect how our "good news" is perceived by others

A solid foundation of truth will insure greater emotional health in the Body of Christ and can save us the pain of discovering our fears were unwarranted all along. Paul encouraged Timothy about the deadliness of those who delude themselves with legends: "Remind them of these things, and solemnly charge them in the presence of God not to wrangle about words, which is useless, and leads to the ruin of the hearers. Be diligent to present yourself approved to God as a workman who does not need to be ashamed, handling accurately the word of truth. But avoid worldly and empty chatter, for it will lead to further ungodliness" (2 Tim. 2:14–17).

Failure to guard ourselves from the spreading of fables and legends has resulted in a climate ripe for error and weakness in the church. God has not given us a spirit of fear, but one of a sound mind. Soundness is necessary in these days of uncertainty. If we are to stand in the face of persecution on every side, we cannot allow fear to dominate our lives, our thinking, and our e-mail.

I believe that as we face our worst fears with the truth of God's Word, we will see less corruption, less deception, and greater tenacity in the church. We may also see more aggressive and fruitful evangelism, for Christians who are sound and strong in the Word will be living epistles of the Word of God.

Jan Brunvand said in his collection of urban legends, *Too Good to Be True,* "If you wanted to invent new urban legends, you might start by imagining ways that people could be led astray by jumping to conclusions."[9]

CHAPTER NINE

The
Misinformation Age
→ ←

D id you hear that Honda could send you a new car—just for
forwarding an e-mail message?

Have you heard about the dying child who needs your help in
fulfilling his last wish?

At least you've heard about the various computer viruses,
which can erase all the files on your hard drive.

If you haven't, welcome to the Misinformation Superhighway.

If you have an e-mail account, you've probably received the
new form of chain letters that describes similar freebies, sad sto-

ries and virus warnings. Chain letters have been the scourge of mailboxes for years. Who hasn't received a letter promising money or good luck to those who copy and mail the letter to others and a curse to those who break the chain? Chain letters have enough text appeal to get the reader to respond to opportunities for good fortune, requests from charities, petitions, and warnings.

Today the Internet has become fertile ground for a new breed of chain letters. Unlike those of the past that required some effort to copy, address, stamp, and mail, these new chain e-mail messages allow us the ability to feel good about ourselves with the click of the mouse. These new chain e-mail letters often contain humorous or inspirational themes. They can include any combination of virus warnings, missing children alerts, parodies, petitions, poems, political commentary, practical jokes, prayer requests, protests, and rumors.

"One of the really interesting things is how willing we are to believe [them]," Kim Brackett, a sociology professor at Auburn University-Montgomery, explained. "The messages usually start out with something like, 'I knew this girl whose friend . . .' It's removed, but not so removed that there is not some believability."

SAD STORIES

Christians worldwide have always been counted on to support individuals in dire need. Who wouldn't be moved if an e-mail message announced you could help fulfill the last dying wish of a sick child with just the push of a button? Sadly, there are those who push the right emotional buttons in us with an endless stream of bogus charities and causes.

One theme often found in chain e-mail letters is the opportunity to help young children with life-threatening diseases. No one is certain as to the origin of these messages of malaise, but they have many variations of the same theme; some have a bit of truth in them, and others are pure rubbish.

Here is a copy of the best example of a little boy's last request:

> Kid's last wish, please help!
>
> Hello!
>
> Craig Shergold is a 7-year-old boy who lives in Keen, N.H. He is dying from an inoperable brain tumor. He made a wish to a children's foundation, that he wants one million get-well cards sent to him by August 15 so that he can be in the World Book of Records before he dies. Cards can be made or bought. Please send the cards to the following address:
> Craig Shergold
> C/O Children's Wish Foundation
> 32 Perimeter Center East
> Atlanta, GA 30346
>
> Please pass this on to ten other people! Come on and help this boy!

The best known of all the health-related chain e-mail letters is the story of a British boy named Craig Shergold. According to a story originating in 1989, Craig was diagnosed with terminal brain cancer. To bolster his spirits, his loved ones came up with an idea to solicit get-well cards (or in some versions business cards) from the around the world in the hopes of landing him in the *Guinness Book of World Records.*

The campaign was a huge success. On occasions the family received up to 10,000 letters a day. In less than a year the plea netted more than 16 million cards, and by 1991 the total reached the 30 million mark. Craig easily landed a new world's record. But it didn't stop there. The cards kept coming.

The publicity surrounding the Guinness record caught the attention of a wealthy American philanthropist, who arranged for

Craig's brain surgery. Most of the malignant tumor was removed, and Craig's cancer went into remission. But the cards kept coming. According to the latest estimate, his family has received more than 150 million cards. As of June 2000, Craig Shergold was a healthy twenty-year-old with a new wish. He wants the cards to stop.

A Royal Mail spokesman said, "We consider this to be a form of harassment. It is a nightmare for the Shergold family, and we would call on people not to respond to chain letters." But with e-mail messages requesting that you forward Craig's first wish to "everyone you know," it's not likely that this wish will ever come true. There seems to be no stopping the Shergold chain letter train.

Mistakenly, many people believed that the Make-A-Wish Foundation of America was the sponsor of Craig's last wish. The Make-A-Wish Foundation disavows on their own Web site ever having anything to do with Craig Shergold or the get-well card appeal legend: "In 1989, a then 9-year-old boy named Craig Shergold wanted to be recorded in the Guinness Book of World Records for receiving the most greeting cards. His wish was fulfilled by another wish-granting organization not associated with the Make-A-Wish Foundation. The time and expense required to respond to these inquiries distracts the Foundation from its efforts on behalf of children with life-threatening illnesses, and more importantly, divulges information that is potentially harmful to a child and his or her family."[1]

The story of Jessica Mydek is a variation of the same chain letter. However this one concerns a young female cancer patient and requests for contributions from a well-known cancer organization. Here is a reproduction of the earliest versions of this "dying child" chain letter:

> Little Jessica Mydek is seven years old and is
> suffering from an acute and very rare case of cere-
> bral carcinoma. This condition causes severe
> malignant brain tumors and is a terminal illness.
> The doctors have given her six months to live.

As part of her dying wish, she wanted to start a chain letter to inform people of this condition and to send people the message to live life to the fullest and enjoy every moment, a chance that she will never have. Furthermore, the American Cancer Society and several corporate sponsors have agreed to donate three cents toward continuing cancer research for every new person that gets forwarded this message. Please give Jessica and all cancer victims a chance.

If there are any questions, send them to the American Cancer Society at acs@aol.com

No one has been able to prove that Jessica Mydek exists. We do know that the e-mail address listed in the message, *acs@aol.com*, does not belong to the American Cancer Society, nor does the organization endorse this or any other chain letter campaign.

From the American Cancer Society's web site there is a response that they encourage readers to copy and reprint. In part it reads:

The American Cancer Society is greatly disturbed by reports of a fraudulent chain letter circulating on the internet which lists the American Cancer Society as a "corporate sponsor" but which has in no way been endorsed by the American Cancer Society. There are several variations of this letter in circulation, including one, which has a picture of "Tickle Me Elmo," and one that is essentially a paraphrase of the letter below.

As far as the American Cancer Society can determine, the story of Jessica Mydek is completely unsubstantiated. No fund-raising efforts are being made by the American Cancer Society using chain letters of any kind. Furthermore, the e-mail address ACS@AOL.COM is inactive. Any

messages to the American Cancer Society should
be instead sent through the American Cancer
Society website at http://www.cancer.org.

This particular chain letter with its heartbreak-
ing story appears to have struck an emotional
chord with online users. Although we are very
concerned that the American Cancer Society's
name has been used to manipulate the online public, we applaud the good intentions of all who participated in this letter. We are pleased to note that
there are so many caring individuals out there and
hope that they will find another way to support
cancer research. Jessica Mydek's story, whether
true or false, is representative of that of many cancer patients who benefit daily from the efforts of
legitimate cancer organizations nationwide.[2]

The Mydek hoax has gone through several transformations.
Copycat chain e-mail letters also list the names of the sufferers as
either David Lawitts or Tamara Martin. They imitate the style of
the Mydek letter so closely that you might conclude the same person wrote them.

By having our sympathies played on, we feel obligated to at
least take the time to forward these letters to everyone we know.
"If it tugs at our hearts at all and it's not going to cost us anything, we go ahead and send it out," Kim Brackett said of these
sentimental appeals. "It's not so far-fetched that people of reasonable intelligence wouldn't believe it could happen."

So how do you recognize a chain e-mail letter? How can you
prevent losing friends and clogging the Internet with this electronic junk mail? They all have a similar pattern with three iden-
tifiable parts:

1.   A hook
2.   A threat
3.   A request

→ 101 ←

The hook is designed to catch your interest and get you to read the rest of the letter. The subject line of your message may read "Make Money Fast" or "Get Rich Quick" or other statements related to making money for little or no work. The subject line or first line of the text could also use warnings like "This is real," "Virus Alert," or "A Little Child Is Dying." Hooks will always play on your emotions.

Most of the threats warn you about the terrible things that will happen if you break the chain. However, some play on greed or sympathy to get you to forward the letter. The body of the message often contains official-sounding titles or names, or uses intimidating technical language to get you to believe it is real. It's not unusual to see the line, "Only a selfish person would not forward this letter."

Finally, there is the request. The old chain letters, for example, asked you to mail a dollar to the top ten names on the letter and then pass it on. The chain e-mail letters simply ask you to "Forward this letter to as many people as possible." Judging by the number of names listing who has received it already, so far no one in the chain has checked the credibility of the message.

To help determine the authenticity of these messages always go back to the originator of the chain and ask about the story. Where did they get it? Is there another source for the story, like a newspaper account or TV report? Do they actually know the person named in the message? I have listed some sources in the back of this book that can be used to verify the latest chain letter hoaxes on the Internet. It would be good to keep these Web sites bookmarked on your Internet browser.

FREE STUFF

By nature, I am a skeptical person. You could say that a skeptic's favorite Bible verse is "In the mouth of two or three *thousand* witnesses let everything be established." So you may understand why I was unconvinced when I received this urgent e-mail message from numerous friends over the last couple of years:

Walt Disney Jr. Greeting

Hello Disney fans,

And thank you for signing up for Bill Gates'
Beta E-mail Tracking.

My name is Walt Disney Jr. Here at Disney we
are working with Microsoft which has just com-
piled an e-mail tracing program that tracks everyone to whom this message is forwarded. It does
this through an unique IP (Internet Protocol)
address log book database. We are experimenting
with this and need your help. Forward this to
everyone you know, and if it reaches 13,000
people, 1,300 of the people on the list will receive
$5,000, and the rest will recieve a free trip for two
to Disney for one week during the summer of
1999 at our expense. Enjoy.

Note: Duplicate entries will not be counted.
You will be notified by e-mail with further instructions once this e-mail has reached 13,000 people.

Your friends,

Walt Disney Jr., Disney, Bill Gates, & the
Microsoft Development Team.[3]

Two things immediately came to my mind after I read the e-
mail. First, I suspected there was no Walt Disney Jr. As I looked
into it further, I discovered that Walt Disney had two daughters
and that his nephew Roy has directed the Disney Company since
Walt's death. Second, I noticed that in each message the word
receive was misspelled. With all the money Microsoft and Disney
have, you would believe they could afford a spell checker.

Maybe the originator of this hoax wanted me to believe that
Disney and Microsoft want to spend $6.5 million dollars just to

test an e-mail tracking program. If it sounds too good to be true, well you know how it goes.

Somewhere in the vastness of cyberspace, someone is busy trying to convince us that major companies have unlimited resources to give away money, clothing, cars, vacations—and more—just by having people forward e-mail messages to friends and family. This idea caters to the new American dream, or should I say *wish*—to get something for nothing.

It could be seen as a new form of lottery. However, instead of money, we invest our time and energy into an empty-handed pursuit. The lottery is really nothing more than a form of gambling. It is a leech that can slowly drain our God-given funds. It only emphasizes man's greed and discontent and should be avoided by all that profess reliance upon the Lord. May it never be said that the only difference between people who pray in church and those who pray in casinos is that the ones who pray in the casinos are really serious!

There have been several e-mail tracking hoaxes over the years. Supposedly large companies like Microsoft, America Online, and even clothing chains have promised to send money to those who will participate in their e-mail tracking program. Various computer authorities from AOL's chief of security to Microsoft's technical staff have declared e-mail tracking "impossible." The truth is, the necessary software hasn't been invented yet and the computing power required to track every mailing in every generation of a successful chain letter is far beyond anything accessible.

There are several versions of the e-mail tracking hoax that promise free goodies. One hoax that has been making the rounds since 1998 partners Microsoft with Nike. The promise this time is free merchandise from Nike for randomly selected participants:

> Dear Student,
>
> We at Nike are of the philosophy that the stronger the body, the stronger the mind. It is because of this philosophy that we are offering

free Nike shoes and clothing as part of a contest
that all of you are invited to participate in.
Microsoft Corp. has developed a new e-mail tracing system and is currently offering us the opportunity to help test their system. With the use of
this new technology, we bring a contest to you.
We ask that you forward this e-mail to your fellow
students.

   After one month of testing the tracing software, we will randomly select 500 names from the
list of recipients and each will be given their
choice of a gift certificate for $120.00 toward any
purchase of Nike shoes or apparel.

   Thank you and good luck.
   Computer systems manager: Alan Whitman
   E-mail: swoosh@nike.com
   Nike Information Management Department:
   Beaverton, OR

Don't bother writing Alan Whitman at Nike; he doesn't exist.
Nike isn't offering merchandise to people who help test Microsoft
software, and the e-mail tracing program still does not exist.

Some of these hoaxes claim you can receive free goods from
well-known clothiers like Abercrombie & Fitch, the Gap, and Old
Navy. Here is a copy of one of the phony promises including
another fictitious name:

   Hello everyone! My name is Amber
McClurkin.

   You have probably heard about the e-mail
from Gap offering free clothes to anyone who will
forward the message on. Well, I am the founder of
Abercrombie & Fitch, and I am willing to make a
better deal with you.

You will receive a $25 gift certificate for every five people you forward this to. This is a sales promotion in order to get our name out to young people around the world.

We believe this project can be a success, but only with your help. Thank you for your support!!

Sincerely,
Amber McClurkin
Founder of Abercrombie & Fitch

When the year 2000 was quickly approaching, the following message sounded like a timely promotion from a well-known candy maker:

Hi. My name is Jeffrey Newieb. I am a marketing analyst for M & Ms chocolate candies based in Hershey, Pennsylvania. As the year 2000 approaches, we want to be the candy of the millennium. As you may already know, the Roman numeral for Y2K is MM. We are asking you to pass on this e-mail to 5 friends. Our tracking device is calculating how many e-mails you send out. Every time it reaches 2000 people, you will receive a free case (100 individual 55gram packs) of delicious M & Ms candies. That means the more people it reaches, the more candy you're going to get. Mmmmmm . . . yummy M & Ms for the year 2000!!

Remember, nothing but bad luck will come your way if you do not share this with at least 5 people!

All lovers of good candy know that the Mars Company, headquartered in McLean, Virginia, makes M&Ms. Hershey candies are headquartered in, of all places, Hershey, Pennsylvania. It sounds like a good promotion leading up to the year 2000. In hindsight perhaps someone should have thought of it.

There are many "something for nothing" legends on the Net, including free computers from IBM, free cases of Coke, offers from an alleged merger of America Online and Microsoft, and free stuff from Bath and Body Works and J. Crew. Unfortunately, all respondents came up empty-handed.

It's important to heed the counsel found in Proverbs 28:19–20: "He who tills his land will have plenty of food, But he who follows empty pursuits will have poverty in plenty. A faithful man will abound with blessings, But he who makes haste to be rich will not go unpunished." Isn't a lottery really just an empty and vain pursuit to "get rich quick"? Jesus said, "Beware, and be on your guard against every form of greed; for not even when one has an abundance does his life consist of his possessions" (Luke 12:15). We must learn to be content in all things, trusting the Lord as our only Provider.

Patrick Crispen's *Urban Legend Combat Kit* Web site offers a wealth of information to help combat Internet chain letters and urban legends. When asked by a reader, "Should you forward the message to all of your friends on the off chance that it just might be true?," or, specifically concerning the redistribution of the dying kid hoax letter, "Who could it hurt?" Crispen responded, "The answer is organizations like Make-a-Wish and the American Cancer Society. Because of hoaxes like these, both organizations are now forced to redirect a significant part of their time and resources to combating these hoaxes. Crispen adds, "Unfortunately, one of the prices of Net citizenship is vigilance—you have to be constantly watching for old hoaxes and urban legends masquerading as new."[4]

COMPUTER VIRUS HOAXES

A time bomb may be ticking silently away in your computer, and you may not even know it. If this bomb is detonated, it could destroy all of your files, your hard drive, and even your computer hardware. This is what most people believe when they hear that a new computer virus is spreading out of control on computers across the world. Like a real virus, you may not know you've been infected until symptoms appear, and by then it may be too late.

A computer virus is a special kind of computer program that is written to create copies of itself and attach these copies to other programs. Working stealthily, these viruses can produce terrible side effects in your computer. On MS-DOS and Windows systems, these files usually have the extensions .EXE, .COM, .BAT, .VBS, or .SYS.

Viruses can infect any computer, from the smallest laptop to the largest corporate mainframe. In order to infect a computer, a virus must have the chance to execute its code. In general, viruses can be transmitted by

- booting a computer with infected floppy disks or other media that users exchange,
- executing an infected program or e-mail attachments, or
- opening an infected file or shareware program.

Many computer viruses exist, yet some of the virus warnings are actually hoaxes. These virus hoaxes are more than mere annoyances, as they may lead some users to ignore all virus-warning messages, leaving them defenseless against a genuine, damaging virus. Rob Rosenberger, the webmaster for a Web site about computer hoaxes, thinks these bogus warnings are designed simply for fright value. "They scare the willies out of you," he said.[5]

In a statement from the Computer Incident Advisory Capability, established in 1989 to provide on-call technical assistance and information to the Department of Energy, "We are spending much more time de-bunking hoaxes than handling real virus incidents."[6]

There is a virus hoax that you may have heard with a distinct Christian flavor. This warning originated in 1998 and is still circulating over the Internet, appearing in mailboxes worldwide. You may have seen a warning that says, "It Takes Guts to Say Jesus."

Virus Warning! If you receive an e-mail titled "It Takes Guts to Say 'Jesus'" DO NOT OPEN IT. It will erase everything on your hard drive. This information was announced yesterday morning from IBM; AOL states that this is a very dangerous virus, much worse than "Melissa," and that there is NO remedy for it at this time. Some very sick individual has succeeded in using the re-format function from Norton Utilities causing it to completely erase all documents on the hard drive. It has been designed to work with Netscape Navigator and Microsoft Internet Explorer. It destroys Macintosh and IBM compatible computers. This is a new, very malicious virus and not many people know about it. Pass this warning along to EVERYONE in your address book and please share it with all your online friends ASAP so that this threat may be stopped. Please practice cautionary measures and tell anyone that may have access to your computer. Forward this warning to everyone that might access the Internet.

Another tactic behind these false virus warnings is to make the message appear to warn you about faulty programs or products provided over the Internet. Since a lot of people aren't yet comfortable using the Internet, imagine what your reaction would be if you heard about a free service used by thousands each day that could corrupt your computer.

A small, family-owned publishing company called Blue Mountain Arts is still feeling the effects of becoming a victim of a malicious virus hoax. Founded in 1971 by Dr. Stephen Schutz and his wife Susan, Blue Mountain Arts is a greeting card publisher based in Boulder, Colorado. They offer free electronic animated and musical greeting cards that can be e-mailed to anyone in the world.

The ninth most popular Web site in the world, Blue Mountain Arts received unwanted notoriety in early 1999 when this message made its first appearance on America Online:

> Subject: Fwd: BLUE MOUNTAIN CARDS VIRUS ALERT!
> Just received a call from family. A friend of theirs opened a card from Blue Mountain Cards and system crashed.
> Do not open Blue Mountain Cards until further notice.
> Virus has infiltrated their system. Pass it on

Because of the power of the Internet to circulate myths, it took only two weeks for this hoax to spread like wildfire. "We think that there are probably tens of thousands or even hundreds of thousands of people who have received this false warning by now," wrote Jared Schutz, the executive director of Blue Mountain Arts. "We are at wits end about how to fight this unseen enemy."[7]

A counter-information campaign seems to have beaten back the fire. Today, every one of its 1 million daily greeting cards contains a message explaining that Blue Mountain cards are safe.

Probably the first thing to notice about a bogus virus warning is the request to "send this to everyone you know." Genuine warning messages from credible sources probably won't use language like that. Next, look for technical sounding language. If the warning contains confusing technical jargon, most individuals would tend to believe the warning is real. For example, the Good Times hoax warns that "if the program is not stopped, the computer's processor will be placed in an nth-complexity infinite binary loop which can severely damage the processor." The first time I read this, it sounded authentic. But with a little research I soon learned that there is no such thing as "an nth-complexity infinite binary loop" and that processors are designed to run loops continuously without damage.

However, computer viruses are too real and often strike without advanced warning. In May 2000 the ILOVEYOU worm struck hundreds of thousands of computers across the world as workers clicked to open an e-mail attachment called "LOVE-LETTER-FOR-YOU.TXT.vbs." Some users reported receiving the same malicious e-mail, but the "I love you" subject line wording was replaced with "Mother's Day confirmation" or "very funny joke."

Nevertheless no one was laughing. An estimate of lost files and computer downtime worldwide was approaching almost $10 billion in the first week of this bug's life. In just five hours, the ILOVEYOU worm swept through the United States, Europe, and Asia, hitting everything from the Pentagon to Parliament.

Richard M. Smith, the programmer who helped nab the author of the 1999 Melissa virus, said he was amazed by how fast the ILOVEYOU e-mail worm was spreading. "It's so enticing. You get a message that says, 'I love you,' and you really want to open up that attachment to see what's going on."[8] The virus spread quickly by users opening the infected file, then the malicious code accessed the Microsoft Outlook address book and sent a copy of itself to every e-mail address entered.

So what can a person do to protect themselves from computer viruses? Experts have several suggestions, but basically you can do three things to inoculate yourself.

1. DON'T DO ANYTHING

Remember, "curiosity" killed the cat and could also crash your computer. A virus is a miniprogram, so if you don't run the program, it can't hurt you. You can simply ignore or delete any file that arrives as an e-mail attachment. The best advice if you do receive an attached file, even from a friend, before you open it ask your friend if they have opened the same file on their computer.

In the meantime, resist the temptation to open a file attachment no matter how cute the name of it might be.

2. USE YOUR ANTIVIRUS SOFTWARE

If you do not currently have antivirus software on your computer, buy some immediately. Good antivirus programs can run automatically as you start your computer each day. Really good programs will alert you when to check their Web site for updates as new breeds of viruses are discovered regularly. Frequently updating your software helps avoid infection.

3. BACK UP YOUR FILES

While antivirus programs can clean an infected machine, they can't restore files that have been corrupted. Experts encourage users to make a complete backup of your computer at least once a month and a daily backup of important files like documents, financial accounts, and important mail. If this is not feasible, at least make a complete backup twice a year and a weekly backup of important files.

There are many resources on the Internet that can identify real and counterfeit computer viruses and explain more clearly how they work. For more information about computer virus hoaxes, refer to a partial list at the end of this book. In today's information age, as more and more people encounter the Internet for the first time, remember: when in doubt, don't send it out.

CHAPTER TEN

The Experts Speak

↗ ↖

Former attorney general of the United States Edwin Meese is credited with a famous line we often quote only in part. Meese drolly observes, "An expert is somebody who is more than 50 miles from home, has no responsibility for implementing the advice he gives, and shows slides."

Experts are stalked by lawyers as key witnesses, by journalists as reliable sources, and the American public seems to hang on their every pronouncement. All through history, experts have offered their opinions on every conceivable subject under the sun. Yet time has often shown many of their estimations, conclusions, and views to be dead wrong. Don't you just love laughing at our own human imperfections? It's one of the few things that can keep us sane in a tough world. Still, it often seems the more trivial the issue, the greater we hold to our contentions and self-assurance of absolute rightness.

PREDICTIONS REGARDING GREAT IDEAS

Here are some examples of the so-called "know-it-all's" most misguided predictions and myth-quotes. Legend and time have attributed these bad predictions as coming from the mouths of people who perhaps should have known better.

"This 'telephone' has too many shortcomings to be seriously considered as a means of communication. The device is inherently of no value to us." Western Union internal memo, 1876

"For the majority of people, smoking has a beneficial effect." Dr. Ian G. Macdonald, Los Angeles surgeon, quoted in *Newsweek*, November 8, 1963

"The wireless music box has no imaginable commercial value. Who would pay for a message sent to nobody in particular?" David Sarnoff's associates' response to his appeal for investments in the radio in the 1920s

"Computers in the future may weigh no more than 1.5 tons." *Popular Mechanics*, 1949

"The concept is interesting and well formed, but in order to earn better than a 'C,' the idea must be feasible." A Yale University management professor's response to Fred Smith's paper proposing reliable overnight delivery service—Smith later founded Federal Express

"We don't like their sound, and guitar music is on the way out." Decca Recording Company executive rejecting the Beatles, 1962

"Stocks have reached what looks like a permanently high plateau." Irving Fisher, professor of economics, Yale University, 1929

"Man will never reach the moon regardless of all future scientific advances." Dr. Lee De Forest, inventor of the vacuum tube and father of television

"Louis Pasteur's theory of germs is ridiculous fiction." Pierre Pachet, professor of physiology at Toulouse, 1872

"The abdomen, the chest, and the brain will forever be shut from the intrusion of the wise and humane surgeon." Sir John Eric Ericksen, British surgeon, appointed Surgeon-Extraordinary to Queen Victoria, 1873

"There is no reason anyone would want a computer in their home." Ken Olson, president, chairman and founder of Digital Equipment Corp., 1977

"This fellow Charles Lindbergh will never make it. He's doomed." Harry Guggenheim, millionaire aviation enthusiast

"There is not the slightest indication that nuclear energy will ever be obtainable. It would mean that the atom would have to be shattered at will." Albert Einstein, 1932

"640K ought to be enough for anybody." Bill Gates, 1981

"It will be years—not in my time—before a woman will become Prime Minister." Margaret Thatcher, 1974

"There will never be a bigger plane built." A Boeing engineer, after the first flight of the 247, a twin-engine plane that carried ten people

"If excessive smoking actually plays a role in the production of lung cancer, it seems to be a minor one." Dr. W. C. Heuper of the National Cancer Institute, as quoted in the *New York Times* on April 14, 1954

"I have traveled the length and breadth of this country and talked with the best people, and I can assure you that data processing is a fad that won't last out the year." The editor in charge of business books for Prentice Hall, 1957

"With over 50 foreign cars already on sale here, the Japanese auto industry isn't likely to carve out a big slice of the U.S. market." *Business Week*, August 2, 1968

"I think there is a world market for maybe five computers." Thomas Watson, chairman of IBM, 1943

"But what . . . is it good for?" Engineer at the Advanced Computing Systems Division of IBM, 1968, commenting on the microchip

"Everything that can be invented has been invented." Charles H. Duell, commissioner, U.S. Office of Patents, 1899

PREDICTIONS FOR THE YEAR 2000

Here are some startling expert predictions from the past that show us all what life will be like living in the new millennium.

"[Using] wonderful new materials far stronger than steel, but lighter than aluminum . . . houses [in the year 2001] will be able to fly. . . . The time may come when whole communities may migrate south in the winter, or move to new lands whenever they feel the need for a change of scenery." Arthur C. Clarke, "The World of 2001," *Vogue*, 1966

"Man in [2000] may be eating 'water flea' steaks as a part of his daily diet. Dr. John R. Olive of Colorado State University said the 'water flea,' Daphnia, is not really a flea at all but a bedbug-sized, soft-shelled crustacean that looks a bit like a tiny clam. Preliminary experiments have shown that a water flea-algae mixture is palatable as soup either cooked or uncooked. The mixture can also be dehydrated into a paste or into dried cakes. 'It has a taste somewhat similar to shrimp,' Dr. Olive said. With just a small amount of flavoring, the mixture can be made to taste like eggs or steak." *Science Digest*, 1961

"Solar powered packs, which will be designed into the shoulders of a garment, will draw energy from the sun and store it. Tubes to distribute this energy will extend from the shoulders through the entire suit. The retentive fibers will heat in the winter and cool in the summer by means of a control system." Fashion designer Larry Le Gaspi, 1981

"[Commuters will] rent small four-seater capsules such as we find on a ski lift. These capsules will be linked together into little trains that come into the city. As the train goes towards the perimeter of the city, the capsule will become an individual unit. One can then drive to wherever he may want to go." Ulrich Frantzen, Prophecy for the Year 2000, 1967

"In the year 2000, we will live in pre-fabricated houses light enough for two men to assemble. . . . [We'll] cook in our television sets and relax in chairs that emit a private sound-light-color spectacular." The *New York Times,* January 7, 1968

"By 2000, the machines will be producing so much that everyone in the U.S. will, in effect, be independently wealthy. With government benefits, even nonworking families will have, by one estimate, an annual income of $30,000–$40,000. How to use leisure meaningfully will be a major problem." *Time,* February 25, 1966

"Pneumatic tubes, instead of store wagons, will deliver packages and bundles. These tubes will collect, deliver and transport mail over certain distances, perhaps for hundreds of miles. They will at first connect with the private houses of the wealthy, then with all homes. Great business establishments will extend them to stations, similar to our branch post offices of today, whence fast automobiles will distribute purchases from house to house." The *Ladies' Home Journal,* December 1900

"By 2000, sawdust and wood pulp will be converted into sugary foods. Discarded paper table 'linen' and rayon underwear will be bought by chemical factories and converted into candy." John Smith, *Science Digest,* 1967

"By 2000, politics will simply fade away. We will not see any political parties." R. Buckminster Fuller, 1966

Here are ten things, besides flying cars, that science fiction writers expected us to have by 2000:

1. Space stations, space liners, rocket planes that take businessmen around the planet in an hour.
2. Nonaddictive mood drugs.
3. Twenty-hour work weeks.

4. Artificial meat made from algae or soybeans that tastes exactly like the real thing
5. Speedy moving sidewalks to transport urban commuters.
6. Laundries that wash, dry, and fold your clothes in seconds.
7. Slower aging, longer life spans, and routine transplants of all body parts.
8. Multilevel city streets to eliminate traffic jams.
9. Underground picture windows that are actually computerized view screens that simulate outdoor scenery.
10. Mechanical pets.[1]

Experts have been acknowledged in every field of endeavor, such as science, math, astronomy, and economics. As 2000 approached, with all those mysterious unknowns, we eagerly sought out those experts in predicting our future, believing only they would show us the way into the new millennium.

GOD'S "PREDICTIONS"

In chapter 3 of his first letter to the church at Corinth, Paul contrasts those who still believe that human wisdom can amount to anything, with those who trust only in the wisdom that comes from the Father. In verse 18, Paul writes, "Let no man deceive himself. If any man among you thinks that he is wise in this age, let him become foolish that he may become wise." His caution is to make sure that the self-important wisdom of this age does not creep into our church. We should always use discernment in our daily life, but discernment must be exercised in love. Love is not boastful or prideful, it doesn't always have to be right or have the last word, and it admits when it's wrong. In this world there will always be people who feel the need to express their opinion on virtually everything. Intellectual pride isn't content to listen quietly and passively. By its nature it must criticize and find fault. It needs to win every debate; it hates opposition or contradiction, and frequently responds to disagreement with looks or words of condescension.

Paul calls on us to forsake the worldly wisdom of this age and to live our lives through the divine wisdom of God. He writes,

"For the wisdom of this world is foolishness before God. For it is written, 'He is THE ONE WHO CATCHES THE WISE IN THEIR CRAFTINESS'; and again, 'THE LORD KNOWS THE REASONINGS of the wise, THAT THEY ARE USELESS'" (1 Cor. 3:19–20).

God's wisdom is the foundation on which we build our lives and the standard for all that we do and think. We must beware of placing our trust in, or taking pride in, the wisdom of men. We need to embrace the wisdom of God, knowing that it alone is true wisdom.

Another thing Paul exhorts us to do is to avoid boasting in men. He says, "So then let no one boast in men. For all things belong to you, whether Paul or Apollos or Cephas or the world or life or death or things present or things to come; all things belong to you, and you belong to Christ; and Christ belongs to God" (1 Cor. 3:21–23).

Because the wisdom of men is foolish and destructive, it is vanity to boast in our own talents, abilities, and wisdom without considering that these are gifts from God. We did not create ourselves, but we were created, formed in his image, and ultimately transformed by renewing our carnal minds. Our boasting is not good, and we do ourselves a great disservice by believing that God's truth can only come from "experts." We all have the same spirit, and all things are ours.

We often put excessive pressure on our pastors and teachers when we see them as experts with all the answers, with the ability to solve all our problems for us. If we allow church leaders, teachers, or experts to become too greatly elevated in our view, they can do almost anything, and large numbers of their followers may trail along unquestioningly. In the church when we idolize our leaders, we may start making excuses for their faults and mistakes. We must remember that leaders are no more than servants, and we are all to be accountable one to another.

The next four chapters in this book demonstrate what has happened throughout church history when we forgot the balance of God's Word and put our confidence only in experts. We will discover the real danger to our Christian witness when we do not call into account those who boldly make extreme assertions and predictions. The repeated failure of some of these experts to accurately predict the future should be a word of warning to all of us:

"Do you see a man wise in his own eyes? There is more hope for a fool than for him" (Prov. 26:12).

CHAPTER ELEVEN

Millennium Fever

➤ ◄

M ount Vesuvius, in Italy, had erupted. Not just once but three times in the last nine years. Surely," wrote the monk Radulfus Glaber, "these are the signs and wonders that foretell the second coming of Christ and the apocalypse."[1]

The end is near! The year is 999.

According to popular lore, Europeans living in the year 999 were more panicked about the Apocalypse than people were in 1999. Allegedly on December 31, 999, lords and peasants knelt in churches together to await Jesus. Crowds of doomsday-fearing penitents gave away their possessions, shut down their businesses, or committed suicide en masse in expectation of the great Judgment Day.

On that fateful New Year's Eve night in 999, the immense basilica of St. Peter's in Rome was crowded for what many believed to be the last midnight mass. As Frederick H. Martens writes in *The Story of Human Life*, there was a dramatic climax at St. Peter's.

> The midnight mass had been said, and a deathly silence fell. The audience waited. . . . Pope Sylvester said not a word. . . . The clock kept on ticking. . . . Like children afraid of the dark, all those in the church lay with their faces to the ground, and did not venture to look up. The sweat of terror ran from many an icy brow, and knees and feet, which had fallen asleep, lost all feeling. Then suddenly—the clock stopped ticking! Among the congregation the beginning scream of terror began to form in many a throat. Stricken dead by fear, several bodies dropped on the stone floor.[2]
>
> The clock continued to strike during the night. It struck one, two, three, and four. A deathly silence still reigned. Then when the clock struck twelve again, Pope Sylvester rose, turned around, and signified to the people the terror had passed. People began to sing hymns of joyful deliverance when the calendar deadline passed and it became clear that the Judgment Day had been deferred. The thousandth year of the birth of Christ had passed without catastrophe.

Other scholars believe the men of the Middle Ages met the change to a new millennium with widespread indifference. They believe the prophecies that predicted the end of the world did not provoke a wave of terror mainly because people at that time did not yet count in centuries and consequently were not aware of the date.

So what actually happened? Historical evidence from this time period is mostly sketchy, but from the book called *Five Histories* written in 1044 by Rodulfus Glaber, a French monk, we find some stories of millennial anticipation. In 989, for example, an unusually bright appearance of what was later named Halley's Comet provoked fear and wonder throughout Europe. Glaber commented on the phenomenon: "Whenever such a prodigy appears to men it clearly portends some wondrous and awe-inspiring event in the world shortly after." Glaber also noted the widespread growth of false religion and the appearance of heretics and false messiahs who attempted to lead the faithful astray. "All this accords with the prophecy of Saint John, who said that the Devil would be freed after a thousand years," Glaber wrote.[3]

Glaber also noted an unusual movement among the peasants known as the Peace of God movement. This movement drew tens of thousands of peasants to open-air gatherings, where they participated in public processions, prayer meetings, and repentance rituals. Though the hope of a thousand years of peace on earth was tied to the millennial anniversary of the birth of Christ, the Peace of God movement did not last long, and failed to prevent future wars.

Important date changes, like the passing from one century to the next, seem to plunge people into feelings of expectation tainted with either dread or hope. With a new millennium around the corner, the interest in apocalypticism in the late 1990s was truly on the rise. Many people interpreted the Y2K computer problem as evidence that modern civilization was on the verge of breakdown. Yet, the uneventful dawning of the year 2000 did not curb our desire for millennial madness. Some doomsayers continued to wait for the other shoe to drop on February 29, 2000, believing that computers could not make the leap into an extra day, while others put off the Apocalypse until January 1, 2001.

WHAT IS MILLENNIALISM?

Millennialism is the biblically based belief in the return of Christ to establish a thousand-year reign of peace. The Book of Revelation, chapter 20, describes a "millennial kingdom," a one-thousand-year period of divine peace on earth that many believe will follow the second coming of Jesus Christ, sort of heaven on earth.

> And I saw an angel coming down from heaven, having the key of the abyss and a great chain in his hand.
>
> And he laid hold of the dragon, the serpent of old, who is the devil and Satan, and bound him for a thousand years,
>
> and threw him into the abyss, and shut it and sealed it over him, so that he should not deceive the nations any longer, until the thousand years were completed; after these things he must be released for a short time.
>
> And I saw thrones, and they sat upon them, and judgment was given to them. And I saw the souls of those who had been beheaded because of the testimony of Jesus and because of the word of God, and those who had not worshiped the beast or his image, and had not received the mark upon their forehead and upon their hand; and they came to life and reigned with Christ for a thousand years.
>
> The rest of the dead did not come to life until the thousand years were completed. This is the first resurrection.
>
> Blessed and holy is the one who has a part in the first resurrection; over these the second death has no power, but they will be priests of God and of Christ and will reign with Him for a thousand years.

And when the thousand years are completed,
Satan will be released from his prison,
    and will come out to deceive the nations which
are in the four corners of the earth, Gog and
Magog, to gather them together for the war; the
number of them is like the sand of the seashore.
    And they came up on the broad plain of the
earth and surrounded the camp of the saints and
the beloved city, and fire came down from heaven
and devoured them.
    And the devil who deceived them was thrown
into the lake of fire and brimstone, where the
beast and the false prophet are also; and they will
be tormented day and night forever and ever.
(Rev. 20:1–10)

According to their "end times" timetable, millennialists fall
into one of three categories. Premillennialists believe that the
return of Christ will be preceded by various signs, including wars,
famines, earthquakes, the preaching of the gospel to all nations, a
great apostasy, the appearance of Antichrist, and the great tribulation. These events will then culminate in the second coming of
Christ, which will result in a thousand-year period of peace and
righteousness with Christ and his saints in command of the world.
Nature will have the curse removed from it—even the desert will
produce abundant crops—Christ will restrain all evil during the
age. At the end of this golden age there will be one final rebellion
of wicked people against Christ and his saints, but God will crush
this rebellion.

Postmillennialists believe that the Millennium will come
through Christian preaching and teaching to the entire world.
This will result in a more peaceful and prosperous world as more
people are converted to Christ. Evil will be held in check as the
moral and spiritual influence of Christians permeates the world.
During this time the church will influence all the arenas of life,

and many of the economic and social problems will be solved. The millennium closes with the second coming of Christ, the resurrection of the dead, and the last judgment.

The third position, amillennialism, states there will be a continuing of both good and evil in the world until the return of Christ. Amillennialists believe that the kingdom of God is established in this world as Christ rules his church through the Word and the Spirit. They believe that the future kingdom refers to the new earth and life in heaven.

BELIEFS OF THE EARLY CHURCH

Millennial beliefs among the first Christians were derived from the Jewish apocalyptic traditions current in the centuries before and after Jesus Christ. Some scholars have, in fact, suggested that in its origins, Christianity was related to such millenarian groups as the Essenes. These millennial teachings were characterized by an apocalyptic interpretation based upon the prophecies of Daniel and the Book of Revelation that point to the supernatural intervention of God in human affairs and the ultimate defeat of the devil.

The early Christians viewed the Millennium mentioned in Revelation as a seven-day "Great Week." This was an inspirational theory established in the first century A.D. by Jewish radicals who claimed time would be brought to an end by the arrival of the Messiah six thousand years from the time of creation.

The theory divided history into seven phases based on the seven days in a week. This concept found in the apocryphal epistle of Barnabas written around A.D. 120 says, "'God finished his work in six days. . . .' That means that in 6,000 years God will bring all things to completion, because for Him, 'a day of the Lord is as 1,000 years . . . .' Therefore, my children, in six days, that is in 6,000 years, the universe will be brought to an end. 'And on the seventh day he rested. . . .'"[4] Though this epistle has not been accepted as part of the New Testament (it also alleges that hyenas change sex every year, and that Judaism sprang from the deceit of a bad angel[5]), this principle, also known as a Sabbatical Millennium, has become accepted by many Christians, as well as end-time prophecy teachers, who believed that the year 2000 was precisely six thousand years since the creation of the world.

Second Peter 3:8 says, "With the Lord one day is as a thousand years, and a thousand years as one day." The interpretation is made that as God created the world in six days, and rested on the seventh, it stands to reason that we have completed the sixth day, or six thousand years since creation, and are entering the seventh and final day, a time of rest on the earth. We do not accurately know the exact age of the world, and without it the date of Christ's return and the beginning of the seventh and final millennium cannot be known.[6]

Christians have passionately anticipated the beginning of this seventh and last millennium, the Sabbath day of rest for the world, throughout church history. During the time Christianity was accepted as the main religion of the Roman Empire, Augustine, bishop of Hippo, expressed an amillennial view that dominated Western Christian thought during the Middle Ages. He believed the prophecies in the Book of Revelation were to be interpreted allegorically. According to his interpretation, the Millennium referred to the church in which Christ reigned with his saints. The spiritual battle had already been won, and Christ had triumphed through the cross. Satan was reduced to lordship over the City of the World, which coexisted with the City of God. During this same period, the Spanish monk Beatus saw only "14 years left to complete the sixth millennium, and therefore presumably only 14 years also until Antichrist's coming."[7]

MILLENNIUM–DATING USING ANCIENT GENEALOGIES

In 1654 Archbishop Ussher of Armagh, Ireland, proposed a theory that by adding up the genealogies from the Bible he could determine that the creation occurred at 9 A.M. on October 26, 4004 B.C. Using Ussher's figures, adding six thousand years to the start of creation would put the start of Christ's thousand-year rule at the end of the twentieth century or the beginning of the twenty-first.

PREMILLENNIAL DISPENSATIONALISM

During the nineteenth century a new element was added to premillennialism: dispensationalism. Edward Irving, a Church of Scotland minister who pastored a congregation in London, was one of the first in the development of the new interpretation. He believed that the second coming of Christ consisted of two stages, the first a secret "catching away" of the saints, or rapture, when Christ meets his church in the air and hides them away before a seven-year period of tribulation, and the second, when Christ appears visibly with his saints after the tribulation to rule on earth for a thousand years.

Irving published numerous works on prophecy and organized the Albury Park prophecy conferences. His apocalyptic exposition found support among the Plymouth Brethren, especially by a man named John Nelson Darby. Darby also taught that the purposes of God dealt with mankind in unique ways, which could be understood as different epochs of time, also referred to as dispensations.

THE U.S. AS THE MILLENNIAL KINGDOM

Also in nineteenth-century America, a form of postmillennialism that equated the United States with the kingdom of God became very popular. Many Protestant ministers spoke about nationalism and manifest destiny by depicting the "golden age" as dependent upon the spread of democracy, technology, and the other "benefits" of Western civilization. Many Americans during this period saw our nation as a highly favored nation, with a divine destiny, an idea that had its roots back in European settlements. The Puritan leaders of New England speculated that America might in fact be the New Zion, offering an example to the world of a redeemed and God-fearing social order. This belief emerged strongly in the millennial strand of the great revival movements of the eighteenth and early nineteenth centuries. It was during World War I, due to President Woodrow Wilson's rhetoric, that many believed America was developing into the instrument for spreading democracy, freedom, and peace around the world.

The most ardent of these believers in civil millennialism was Hollis Read, an ordained minister in the Congregational church in Park Street Church, Boston. In his two-volume work, *The Hand of God in History,* Read demonstrated that the increase in our understanding of geography, politics, education, the arts, and morality all pointed to the coming of the fulfillment of the kingdom millennium in America in the nineteenth century. From this base, the golden age would spread to the entire earth. He cited the pervasiveness of the English language, which he claimed made it easier to preach the Word, as one example of the benefits of Western culture.

FALSE PREDICTIONS

Throughout the nineteenth century, the Sabbatical Millennium concept was accepted without question by most English-speaking Protestants. However, history has shown the excesses as well as the attractiveness of millennial thinking. Believers have often abused these views by falsely predicting dates for the end of the world and the return of Christ.

In his 1979 book, *Christ Returns by 1988: 101 Reasons Why,* author Colin Deal uses the six-thousand-year dating theory as proof that the Rapture could take place in 1988 or before. The late Bible teacher and author Lester Sumrall also said in his book, *I Predict 2000 A.D.,* "I predict the absolute fullness of man's operation on planet Earth by the year 2000 A.D. Then Jesus Christ shall reign from Jerusalem for 1000 years."[8]

Author and prophecy lecturer J. R. Church, who wrote the 1986 book *Hidden Prophecies in the Psalms,* draws a parallel between the number of each biblical psalm and the years of the 1900s; Psalm 48 relates to events in 1948, and so on. In the book, Church also uses the Sabbatical Millennium concept to predict the Rapture in 1988. He confirmed, "The Son of God will soon appear to establish a heavenly throne on earth. The next thousand years will be paradise."[9]

Prophecy writer Mary Relfe uses Ussher's research to prove the timing of Christ's return in her book *When Your Money Fails.* "It doesn't take a genius to see that God has allotted man 6,000 years to do his work, and the seventh thousand-year period will be God's Sabbath, the Millennium Reign of Government of Christ . . . . Though much scholarly work has subsequently been done, [Ussher's] timetable remains virtually unchanged."[10]

AMERICAN MILLENNIALISM

William R. Garrett, a professor of sociology at Saint Michael's College in Colchester, Vermont, believes some are merely taking advantage of America's millennial beliefs. He clarified his thoughts this way: "We may have passed the year 2000 two years ago [referring to the common scholarly opinion that Jesus was born in 4 B.C.]. Given that problem, I would say this is an excuse, an opportunity for a lot of folks to say things they want to say."[11]

As the year 2000 approached, about one hundred Americans moved to Jerusalem, anticipating a cataclysm at the end of 1999. According to Brenda E. Brasher, assistant professor of religion at Mount Union College in Alliance, Ohio, "The number of millennial forces at work in our society now are such that it would be surprising if we did not see a certain number of these incidents." The Israeli government committed $12 million to upgrade security at the Temple Mount, fearing extremists might undertake suicide attacks in Jerusalem as a way to bring about the fulfillment of end-times prophecy.

Brasher surveyed several evangelical churches and discovered a different emphasis as the end of the millennium drew near. "I am finding an increase in millennial rhetoric with a kind of intensity to it, and a lot of fear associated with it," she says. "I'm also finding some level heads in those congregations that are trying to balance out or cancel that kind of fear.

"There's an escalating amount of millennial tensions," Brasher says. "Y2K is a lightning rod that's drawing some of this millennial fear. It's an emergent problem where some of this millennial fear can coalesce."[12]

MILLENNIAL VIEWS OF OTHER GROUPS

The idea that all earthly governments will ultimately be overthrown and replaced by a divinely instituted order is an old one, and is not exclusive to Christianity. Muslims believe in the Qur'anic teaching of "the Hour," in which the prophet Jesus returns to earth and God judges mankind. Buddhist scriptures teach of a coming age governed by Maitreya, a Buddha who will be reborn in a period of decline to renew the teachings of Buddhism. Hinduism looks to the end of an age known as the Kali Yuga, which will feature widespread destruction and the final avatar (incarnation) of the god Vishnu on earth. In the late nineteenth century, Native American prophets created the Ghost Dance religion, which anticipated the overthrow of the rule of white people and the restoration of the land to its original inhabitants.

Millennialism is not an exclusive concept used only by the world's religious. Political movements such as Communism and Nazism share many characteristics of religious millennial movements. Nazi leader Adolf Hitler promised his followers that Germany would reign for one thousand years.

PROBLEMS WITH DATING

Yet, there was one small problem when it came time to celebrate the year 2000. No one was certain when the new millennium really began. Some say the new millennium began on January 1, 2000; others say it will begin on January 1, 2001. This conventional view of marking dates is backed by the Library of Congress, the National Bureau of Stands and Technology, and the Royal Greenwich Observatory in Cambridge, England, which say that the first day of the third millennium falls on January 1, 2001. Other scholars argued that the new millennium already passed us by years ago.

Part of the problem is that our modern calendar did not start with a year "zero." You can give credit, or discredit, for the modern calendar to a sixth-century monk named Dionysius Exiguss, known as Dennis the Short. Dennis was commissioned by Pope St. John I to compile a new Easter cycle. Using the standard practice of the day, Dionysius began his countable years with the foundation of Rome. He then divided time again by estimating Christ's birth at 753 A.U.C. (A.U.C.—the founding of Rome). Dennis then restarted time on January 1, 754 A.U.C., eight days after Christ's birth, the feast of circumcision, and coincidentally New Years Day in Roman and Latin Christian calendars.[13]

Most modern scholars agree that Dennis made grave mistakes. Using the Gospels of Matthew and Luke as guides in calculating the birth of Christ, he determined that Jesus was born the year Herod the Great died. Most scholars agree Herod died in 750 A.U.C. The contemporary historian Flavian Josephus reported the death of Herod to have definitely occurred shortly after the lunar eclipse of March 12 and 13, 4 B.C. For Jesus and Herod to overlap, Jesus would have been born in 4 B.C. or earlier. Although no one is certain when Jesus was born, the generally accepted date is somewhere between 8 and 4 B.C.

Dennis' second mistake was he started marking time again on January 1, in the year 1 A.D. (Anno Domini—"in the year of the Lord") and not with the year zero. During the year that Jesus was one year old, the time system that supposedly started with his birth was two years old. For example, babies are zero years old until their first birthday, so modern time was one year old at its inception.[14]

Accordingly, since we started with year 1, the first year was completed at the end of year 1, the first century at the end of A.D. 100, the first millennium at A.D. 1000, and the second millennium at the end of A.D. 2000. By this account, as of January 1, 2001, we will have completed exactly two thousand years since the birth of Christ, and will be ready to enter the third millennium.

Using the latitude given us by the best "guesstimates" as to the birth of Christ, we extrapolate that two thousand years (from the period January 1, 8 B.C. through December 31, 4 B.C.) fell from January 1, 1993 through December 31, 1997. Take into account there was no year zero; so, the second millennium, or two thousand years from the birth of Christ, was more than likely accomplished by December 31, 1997.

But not all people on the earth mark time with the same calendar. A number of cultures have their own calendars separate and distinct from the B.C./A.D. framework. Here is a summary of some of these alternatives:

China: For the estimated 1.2 billion Chinese in this world, the year 2000 was the year 4698 by the Chinese lunar calendar, or the seventeenth year in the seventy-eighth cycle. Developed by Emperor Huang Ti in 2600 B.C., the calendar begins at the second new moon after the winter solstice.

Jews: The Hebrew calendar is a lunar calendar that dates to 3760 B.C. According to tradition the Jewish date their calendar from creation; and the year 2000 was their year 5760.

Muslims: The Muslim calendar begins when Mohammed moved from Mecca to Medina in A.D. 622 and follows the cycles of the moon rather than the sun, making their year only 354 days long. The year 2000 was their year 1421.

Buddhists: The Thereveda Buddhist calendar dates from 544 B.C., the commonly accepted date of Buddha's death. Thereveda Buddhists celebrate the New Year in mid-April.

Hindus: Hindus are in the middle of a calendar cycle that will end in the world's destruction; but that predicted destruction is still 350,000 years away.

Until the end really does come, there will always be those who will set dates, make predictions, write books, and try to convince us the end is near. But if we can learn from the Y2K worries and predictions that didn't pan out, then we will be less likely to be misled in the future. History has proven the doomsday predictions over the past two thousand years 100 percent wrong.

Those who have succumbed to millennial madness throughout history have ended up making unsafe decisions, from selling their possessions to leaving their family and friends. Not only was there the likelihood of damaging the faith of new or immature believers, but also, the cause of Christ was hindered. Though it is possible we are living in the last days, it could be possible that Christ's second coming is a long way off. As Mark 13:32–37 makes clear:

> "But of that day or hour no one knows, not even the angels in heaven, nor the Son, but the Father alone.
> "Take heed, keep on the alert; for you do not know when the appointed time is.
> "It is like a man, away on a journey, who upon leaving his house and putting his slaves in charge, assigning to each one his task, also commanded the doorkeeper to stay on the alert.
> "Therefore, be on the alert—for you do not know when the master of the house is coming, whether in the evening, at midnight, at cock-crowing, or in the morning—
> "lest he come suddenly and find you asleep.
> "And what I say to you I say to all, 'Be on the alert!'"

Our God lives in the past, present, and future. Our concept of time and calendars mean nothing to him. Yes, we know we are "in the season" for the coming of the Lord, but every generation believed that. Our only hope is to completely trust him, to anticipate his coming daily, and work as if it will not happen for a thousand years.

CHAPTER TWELVE

The End
of the World

➔ ←

The Bible contains many unfulfilled prophecies about the
future. The Books of Revelation, Daniel, and Ezekiel, in particular, talk at length about the return of Jesus Christ to this earth
and events leading to the end of this world as we know it. Over
the years, countless individuals have attempted to predict the various end-time events. Among these events are the precise date of
the return of Jesus, the beginning of the battle of Armageddon,
the rapture of the church, and the exact chronology of events
leading to the end of this age and into Christ's millennial reign.

With the coming of the new millennium, many Christians' interests in such matters were on the rise. The *Trends Research Institute* predicted in 1988 that the prophecy business would boom as millennium fever spread throughout most of the world. Just as there is an allure to accurately name the Antichrist, there is an equal attraction to predicting exactly when and how end-time events will unfold. The real tragedy is how many Christian legends have grown out of such a fascination. Let's look back on some predictions from the past that never panned out.

A.D. 156

Montanus, along with followers Prisca and Maximilla, fell into trances and taught that the New Jerusalem was about to descend to an obscure region of Phrygia, now modern day Turkey. Montanus declared himself to be the "Spirit of Truth," the personification of the Holy Spirit mentioned in the Gospel of John, who was about to reveal all truth. He quickly gathered followers and began to spread what Montanists called "The Third Testament," a series of revelatory messages that foretold of the soon-coming Kingdom of God. As word was spread, believers were urged to come to Phrygia to await the Second Coming. So strong was this movement, called Montanism, that it briefly threatened to supplant orthodox Christianity. Whole communities were sharply divided, and discord was the rule when this New Jerusalem didn't appear. Montanus and Maximilla may have voluntarily been martyred as a result, and suicide became linked in the public mind to apocalyptic disappointment, as it is today. Finally, in A.D. 431, the Council of Ephesus condemned the belief in the Millennium as a dangerous superstition, and Montanus was declared to be a heretic.[1]

A.D. 350

Martin of Tours, bishop of Gaul, wrote, "There is no doubt that the Antichrist has already been born. Firmly established, already in his early years, he will, after reaching maturity, achieve supreme power."[2]

A.D. 410

St. Augustine of Hippo recorded an outbreak of panic in Constantinople in A.D. 398, a year he believed marked the completion of 365 years from the Crucifixion. At that time there was a wicked pagan legend circulating that claimed St. Peter had done a deal with the devil that Christianity would last only 365 years.

An earthquake later struck, sending people fleeing to the church. "Everyone, almost with violence, demanded baptism from whom he could," reports Augustine. "Not only in church, but also in their homes and through the streets and squares there was a cry for the saving sacrament, that they might escape wrath."[3]

When during this same time period Rome was sacked by the Visigoths, some proclaimed, "Behold, from Adam all the years have passed, and behold, the 6,000 years are completed."

A.D. 1186

In the 1180s, the time of the Third Crusade, anti-Muslim prophecies believed to have come from astrologers in Spain, telling of a "new world order," began to circulate in Western Europe. One of the messages, the "Letter of Toledo," appearing in 1186, spoke in nightmarish details of events to come in September 1186. "A strong and very powerful wind will arise in the western regions, blackening the air and corrupting it with a poisonous stench. The death and infirmity will seize many, and clanging and cries will be heard in the sky, terrifying the hearts of listeners. In the West discord will also arise and insurrections will occur among the people. There will be one among them who will gather innumerable armies and will make war along the seashore; in this war such a massacre will take place that the force of the spilled blood will be equal to the rising waves."[4]

When the Toledo Letter reached England, the Archbishop of Canterbury ordered a three-day fast. Even after the deadline passed, the letter continued to circulate throughout Europe for centuries, and, like today's predictions, was updated with changing dates and other details.

A.D. 1260

Joachim of Fiore was an apocalyptic thinker who was convinced that the onslaughts of the crusaders corresponded to the sixth seal of Revelation. According to his prophecies, the world was supposed to pass through the reign of Antichrist and enter the Age of the Holy Spirit. He indicated that by the end of the twelfth century the Antichrist was already born in Rome.[5]

Joachim wrote in his *Expositio in Apocalypsia* that history was to be divided into three ages: the Age of the Law (the Father), the Age of the Gospel (the Son), and the final Age of the Spirit. His belief in a golden age that comes at the end of the age, known as Joachimism, still influences many prophetic teachers to this day.

A.D. 1420

In a city near Prague, Martinek Hauska led a following of priests to announce the soon second coming of Christ. They warned everyone to flee to the mountains because between February 1 and February 14, 1420, God was to destroy every town with Holy Fire, thus beginning the Millennium. Hauska's band then went on a rampage to "purify the earth" by ridding the world of "all the false clergymen" in the church. They occupied an abandoned fortress and defied the religious powers of the day, ultimately succumbing to the Bohemians in 1452.[6]

A.D. 1526

Leaders of the Anabaptists in St. Gallen, Switzerland, excited by events of the day, began running through the streets shouting that the Last Day would arrive in exactly one week. Many were baptized, stopped work, abandoned their homes, and set off into the hills, singing and praying in expectant enthusiasm. After a week had passed with no sign of their returning Lord, they returned to their homes.[7]

A.D. 1656

This is the date the world would end according to predictions by Christopher Columbus in his *Book of Prophecies*. Columbus believed that his explorations were the fulfillment of prophecy and that he was to have led a Christian army in a great final crusade that would eventually convert the entire world to Christendom.[8]

THE 1700S

Jonathan Edwards, the theologian and Congregationalist minister whose sermons led to the religious revival known as the Great Awakening, was fascinated by the Apocalypse. He noted all signs of the times, and calculated and recalculated the end's coming. He concluded that Antichrist's rule would end when the papacy ended in 1866, and that the old serpent, the devil, would finally be vanquished in the year 2000, when the Millennium would begin.[9]

1843

One of the most significant figures to come out of the Second Great Awakening was a farmer from upstate New York named William Miller. Miller, a student of the Bible, believed he had a new understanding of how to interpret prophecy, especially the Book of Revelation. Earlier teachers saw the Book of Revelation as an unfolding story with some of the events having already occurred in Christian history. To Miller, nothing in the book had been fulfilled.

Miller believed that the prophecies in the Book of Daniel would be fulfilled in the end, when the second coming of Christ, or what he called the Advent, would occur. His Adventists movement, as it was known, contended that the second coming of Christ would occur in 1843, and according to Miller's interpretation of the Book of Revelation, the new Millennium would then begin. This interpretation, where the thousand-year reign of Christ begins after his return, became known as premillennialism.

This influential new development in American religious history still is widely held to this day.

Like our world today, mass communication and mass marketing made it possible for the Millerite movement to gain momentum. The high-speed printing press was very much used in pamphlets, newsletters, newspapers, and colored charts that illustrated Miller's system. Miller didn't consider himself a great preacher or evangelist; in fact, in his meetings that attracted many thousands, Miller lectured as he would walk people through his new system. Miller convinced his followers that Christ would return sometime between March 21, 1843, and March 21, 1844.

The failure of this prediction in 1843 was called the First Disappointment, and many left the movement. Undaunted, some Millerites, led by Samuel Snow, outlined a new chronology after they realized that Miller had made an error of one year by neglecting to take into account the transition from B.C. to A.D. Miller did not endorse this new theory until the beginning of October 1844, when he announced that "if He (Jesus) does not come within 20 or 25 days, I shall feel twice the disappointment I did this spring."[10]

So with the date changed to October 1844, the excitement was extended for one more year. As the new date approached, as many as fifty thousand followers sold all of their property, refused to plow their fields, and gave away all of their earthly possessions.

But then came what is known as the Great Disappointment. When Christ failed to return the following year, thousands of believers returned to their former churches dismayed, weeping, and feeling untold disillusionment. Despite the best calculations, the world went on as before. In a book published in 1924 about the Adventists movement, the Millerites related how they suffered great ridicule when their prophecies did not come true: "The world made merry over the old prophet's predicament. The taunts and jeers of the 'scoffers' were well-nigh unbearable. If any of Miller's followers walked abroad, they ran the gauntlet of merciless ridicule. What!—Not gone up yet?—We thought you'd gone up! Aren't you going up soon?—Wife didn't go up and leave you behind to burn, did she?"[11]

1914, 1918, 1920, 1925, 1941, 1975, AND 1994

Even cults and sects have attempted to predict the end of the world. These are the dates for the end of the world as predicted by the Jehovah's Witnesses (Watchtower Bible and Tract Society). When the first date of 1914 didn't come to pass, they blamed it on their misinterpretation of Psalm 90:10 as defining the length of a generation to be eighty years. Add eighty years to 1914 and you get 1994, their most recent erroneous prediction. Another estimate was set to be six thousand years after the creation of Eve, for which no date can be determined with any accuracy. The *Watchtower* magazine quoted a pastor from California, Mihran Ask, as saying in January 1957 that "sometime between April 16 and 23, 1957, Armageddon will sweep the world! Millions of persons will perish in its flames and the land will be scorched."[12] The Jehovah's Witnesses are no longer setting dates, but expect the end of the world, as we know it, at any time.

1988

This year was a pivotal point for apocalyptic predictions for two reasons. In his 1970 best-seller, *The Late Great Planet Earth,* author Hal Lindsey implied that 1988, forty years from the refounding of the nation of Israel, would be the year to set in motion the key events in the apocalypse. Lindsey illustrated his calculations by using Jesus' parable of the fig tree in Matthew 24:32:

> When the Jewish people, after nearly 2000 years of exile, under relentless persecution, became a nation again on 14 May 1948, the "fig tree" put forth its first leaves.
>
> Jesus said that this would indicate that He

was "at the door," ready to return. Then He
said, "Truly I say to you, this generation will
not pass away until all these things take place"
(Matt. 24:34).

What generation? Obviously, in context, the
generation that would see the signs—chief among
them the rebirth of Israel. A generation in the
Bible is something like forty years. If this is a cor-
rect deduction, then within forty years or so of
1948, all these things could take place. Many
scholars who have studied Bible prophecy all their
lives believe that this is so.[13]

The same conviction was expressed in the title of another
book by Lindsey, *The 1980's: Countdown to Armageddon*. In the
preface Lindsey writes: "Many people will be shocked by what
will happen in the very near future. The decade of the 1980s
could very well be the last decade of history as we know it."[14]

The idea of relating end-time events to the fortieth anniversary
of either Israel's "rebirth" as a nation or the taking of Jerusalem in
1967 is shared by many other end-time authors. David Webber
and Noah Hutchings reveal the same conviction as Lindsey in
their book *Is This The Last Century?* They write: "Forty is the
Jewish number for testing. Since Israel was refounded as a nation
in 1948, she has been tested like no other nation has been tested
before. . . . The Bible indicates that Israel will be tested until the
Messiah comes. Forty years from 1948 is 1988."[15]

As a young student at UCLA in the late sixties, Chris Hall,
vividly recalls the deeply felt urgency of the times. He remembers,
"Many students sensed they stood on the edge of history; discussions and debates, religious or not, often had an apocalyptic tone.
The world seemed tilted on edge, off-kilter, out of balance. The
conflict over the war in Vietnam revealed cracks in American
moral underpinnings, at least from the perspective of the young.
Students opposed to the war insisted that it end immediately.

Others felt just as strongly that those opposing the war were disloyal, cowardly sentimentalists, unaware of political realities. Whether for or against the war, many students sensed that life in America was changing: politically, morally, spiritually."

It was in this setting that Hall first heard the gospel from a former tugboat captain, Hal Lindsey. In an article published in the October 25, 1999, edition of *Christianity Today,* Hall shares why he has never forgotten the lessons learned from Lindsey's research. "Every Wednesday night, students from UCLA gathered at the Light and Power House, a former college fraternity house on the fringes of the campus, to hear Hal teach the Bible. Some students came from evangelical backgrounds. Many more were from nominal Christian or secular homes. Hal, often dressed in a tank top, blue jeans, and leather boots, walked us through the Bible. I recall, almost wistfully, the sense of excitement, intensity, and urgency we felt as Hal linked the Scripture to our world, our dilemmas, our questions. He possessed a gift for linking the simplicity of the gospel to our longing for truth and our interest in discerning how Christ's work and words were connected to life in the wacky world of the sixties. And of course, Hal's interest in biblical prophecy fed into the wider apocalyptic fervor of the youth culture and American culture at large," Hall writes.

"Hal had unexpectedly uncovered a deep vein of eschatological and apocalyptic longing in the fundamentalist/evangelical subculture and in American culture at large. Over a period of years, the energy of the Jesus movement spent itself, I think, largely because of the failure to develop structures to accommodate and nurture the thousands coming into the kingdom. Also, significant moral confusion characterized the movement as a whole in its waning years. We had spent countless hours analyzing and identifying the time of the Tribulation, the identity of the Antichrist, and whether the church would be raptured before, during, or after the Tribulation.

"Important questions all, but deadly if contemplated ahistorically or in the midst of moral confusion. What was most significant, we had cut ourselves off from the very community—Christ's body the church—that could teach us how to live wisely and sanely as we waited for our Lord and provide the social context necessary for the developing, nurturing, and shaping of Christian character. We wanted our cake (Jesus to return) and to eat it too (to live however we wanted until he came back). Finally, this divorce between eschatology and ethics blew up in our faces."[16]

Garry Friesen echoed the same sentiments in an issue of *Moody Monthly*. Looking back, Friesen reassessed *The Late Great Planet Earth* as Israel's forty-year anniversary approached. He noted, "Rereading *Late Great*, however, has reminded me of its power. It communicated a complex subject so well that both believers and unbelievers kept turning the pages and opening their Bibles."[17] With more than 35 million copies sold worldwide, only the Bible itself has outsold Lindsey's simple, dispensational, premillennial explanation of the church's hope for Christ's return.[18]

But in striking comparison to *The Late Great Planet Earth*, a fifty-eight-page pamphlet from retired NASA engineer Edgar Whisenant became a controversial best-seller in Christian bookstores around the country. Whisenant elaborated upon Hal Lindsey's generational timetable to come up with *88 Reasons Why the Rapture Will Be in 1988*.

But Whisenant also employed several different methods to support his claim that the Jewish Feast of Trumpets or "Rosh Hash-Ana 1988 must be the time of the Church's Rapture." He was so certain that he had nailed the deadline that he said, "Only if the Bible is in error am I wrong, and I say that unequivocally." According to his calculations the time for the rapture was a three-day window from September 11 to 13, 1988, with the beginning of World War III at sunset October 3.

This excerpt from his book shows that "Reason #76" uses the ancient theory of the Sabbatical Millennium to prove his case.

There is a direct correlation between the
seven-days of creation and the number of years of

man's existence. Ps. 90:4 says that 1000 years is as a day to the Lord. II Pet. 3:8 says that one day is as 1000 years to the Lord (and 1000 is as one day). Heb. 4:4–6 & 9 say that the Lord's day of rest on the seventh day of creation equals the 1000 years of Millennial rest for His people. If the seventh day of the Lord's creative week is 1000 years, then the other six days of creation must be 1000 years, each for a total of 7000 years. Bible history and genealogical [sic] tables show that from Adam to Jesus was 4000 years. Since the last 1000 years of the 7000 represents the millennial rest, Jesus should return 6000 years from the birth of Adam.

The Chronological Bible gives Adam's creation by God as Friday 3975 B.C., and states that Adam was created at approximately 30 years of age. So 3975 B.C. less 30 years equals 4005 B.C. as the year that Adam would have been born, had Adam been born of a woman. And from 4005 B.C. to 1995 A.D. are 6000 years or six days with God, and the year that the seventh day (called the Millennium) would be expected to start. So if the Millennium would start in 1995, then the 70th week of Daniel [the time of the Tribulation, preceded by the Rapture] would have to start in 1988 in order to be completed on time.[19]

The book came out only a few months before the date of the predicted Rapture was to take place, and for what little time the book had, it made quite an impact on the Christian media. Christian bookstore owners couldn't keep up with the demand. According to the October 12, 1988, issue of *Christianity Today*, 3.2 million copies were printed, with an attempt made to distribute it to every pastor in America. His calculations caused such a commotion that his pamphlet was used as sermon material in many evangelical churches.

The Trinity Broadcasting Network preempted their *Praise the Lord* show on the nights of September 11–13 for special broadcasts designed to inform nonbelievers of what to do when they found themselves left behind.

Prophecy teacher Charles Taylor planned his 1988 tour of Israel to coincide with Whisenant's date, with the possibility of being raptured from the Holy Land as an incentive: "only $1,975 from Los Angeles or $1,805 from New York (and return if necessary)."[20]

When the end didn't come as predicted, many Christian leaders publicly recanted their endorsements. But Whisenant remained resolute. In true Millerite style, Whisenant claimed his calculations were one year off, so in 1989 he came out with a revision, *The Final Shout: Rapture Report 1989,* this time listing eighty-nine reasons why the Rapture would occur that year. Whisenant explained in chapter 1, "What Went Wrong in 1988—and Why": "My mistake was that my mathematical calculations were off by one year. . . . Since all centuries should begin with a zero year (for instance, the year 1900 started this century), the first century A.D. was a year short, consisting of only 99 years. This was the one-year error in my calculations last year. The Gregorian calendar (the calendar used today) is always one year in advance of the true year. Numbered correctly from the beginning, i.e., 1 A.D., 1989 Gregorian would be only one thousand nine hundred eighty eight years of 365.2422 days each."[21]

The new date calculates "September 1, 1989, as the most likely time for the Rapture, plus or minus one day."[22] Should that date pass without fulfilling his prediction, Whisenant had another contingency plan. "If September 1, 1989, comes and goes, and there is no Rapture, then the next date we should look for would be September 30, 1989."[23]

"If that date passes, and the rapture still does not occur, I believe we have to move the whole sequence of events forward another year to Rosh-Hashanah 1990."[24] But if those dates did not bring the Rapture of the Saints, Whisenant used the same charts used in predicting 1989 to allow the Rapture to occur anywhere from 1990–1993.

Due to his failed prediction the year before, Whisenant's credibility among evangelical and fundamentalist Christians had been damaged beyond repair, and few people took notice of his new effort. This book sold only a small percentage of his prior release, and after a second failed prediction, Whisenant dropped into obscurity.

1994

Harold Camping, the host of "Open Forum" and "Family Bible Study," and president of Family Stations, Inc., startled his listeners in 1992 with a detailed prediction of the return of Jesus and the end of the world. Like several prophecy teachers, his dates coincide with major Jewish feast days like Yom Kippur and the Feast of Tabernacles, but his calculations were more complex, using various chronologies and theories such as the cycles of Jubilee years and the Sabbatical Millennium. In the conclusion of his book *1994?*, Camping specifies a reasoned argument—similar to the millennial calculations of the Millerites and Edgar Whisenant.

> So we see that 2007 B.C. when Jacob was born is indeed a very significant day insofar as being a beginning for 4000 years. And 2007 B.C. followed by 4000 years ends on—yes, that's right—on the year 1994 A.D. How significantly every path we follow using the prophetic numbers of the Bible focuses on 1994 A.D.
>
> We have thus seen that the 390 days during which Ezekiel was to be a type or figure bearing the wrath of God is pointing to the 3900-year period beginning in the year 1907 B.C. when Jacob's name was changed to Israel and continu-

ing to 1994 A.D. On the other hand the forty days Ezekiel was to be a type or figure bearing the wrath of God is pointing to the 4000-year period beginning in the year 2007 B.C. when Jacob was born and also continuing to 1994 A.D.

The fact that both the 390-day prophecy and the forty-day prophecy must end at the same time—Judgment Day—gives us vast assurance that we understand the Scriptures correctly when we see the end as 1994 A.D.

Jesus was born on or about the Day of Atonement. Since in a spiritual sense He is our Jubilee in that all of the blessings of the jubilee year are completed in Him, it would have been very appropriate if He had been born on the beginning day of a jubilee year. . . . We also saw that even though God does not precisely detail the time of Jesus' birth, it had to be fairly close to, and could have been on, the Day of Atonement, 7 B.C., which is within the possibilities allowed by Scripture.

If this is true, then his second coming on the Day of Atonement, September 15, 1994, is entirely reasonable. This will be precisely, to the very day, forty jubilee periods after His birth.

For all these reasons we wonder if September 15 is the date of His return. However, a day during the Feast of Tabernacles is also a distinct possibility. . . . Remember that the term "last day" is found only eight times in the Bible. . . .[Six] of these citations identify with the end of the world, which must come on the last day of the world's existence. Amazingly, or maybe not so amazingly, the two remaining citations are both used in connection with the Feast of Tabernacles. . . . We, therefore, must consider the possibility of Christ's return on one of the days of the Feast of Tabernacles for the year 1994, which will be the period from September 20 to September 27. . . .

Anyone who decides that he does not believe in the fact that the end is so close can do so, but he will be like the proverbial ostrich that sticks his head in the sand. His unbelief will not in any way change the reality of the fact of Christ's return.[25]

In March 1993, Camping appeared on CNN's *Larry King Live*. When King asked, "On a scale of one to ten, how sure are you that Christ is coming in 1994?" Camping replied, "At least nine."[26]

1995

In 1992, David Koresh, of the Branch Davidian group in Waco, Texas, changed the name of their commune from Mt. Carmel to Ranch Apocalypse because of his belief that the final all-encompassing battle of Armageddon mentioned in the Bible would start at the Branch Davidian compound. They had calculated that the end would occur sometime in 1995. In April 1993, after a fifty-one-day standoff against federal agents, seventy-six members of the cult died as a result of what the government claims was a deliberately set fire, and which many citizens believe the government carelessly or deliberately set.

1998

About 150 followers of a Taiwanese Christian-Buddhist spiritual sect, God's Salvation Church, moved into Garland, Texas, a suburb in northern Dallas, to await God's arrival. They believed that on March 25, God would broadcast a commercial on Channel 18 in Garland. God would then be reincarnated into a man on March 31 at 10:00 A.M. They anticipated a crowd of about one million who would want to be touched by God. Their leader, Hon-Ming Chen, selected Garland because it sounded like "God land."

1999

In the early 1990s, the movement known in Korea as "Hyoo-Go" (Rapture) or "Jong Mal Ron" (End Times Theory) was gaining so much acceptance in many Korean Christian denominations that some pastors of mainline Protestant denominations were caught up in the excitement. The movement started in 1997 when Lee Jang-Rim claimed in his book *Getting Close to the End*, that the Rapture would take place on October 28, 1992. Rim, an associate minister at a conventional Protestant church, interviewed Korean children and adults who claimed to have had visions of the Rapture in 1992.

When many of these "visionaries" were excommunicated from their church, Jang-Rim founded the largest of the Korean Rapture sects, Tami Church, better known in the English-speaking world by the title "Mission for the Coming Days." In a full-page ad published in *USA Today* on October 20, 1991, the group showed their adherence to apocalyptic millennialism: "God created the universe in six days and rested on the seventh day, and sanctified the seventh day to be His Day (Gen. 2:3). According to 2 Peter 3:8, 'with the Lord one day is as a thousand years, and a thousand years as one day,' one day can be interpreted as a thousand years. Therefore, human history will end in six thousand years, and Jesus will reign in the last thousand years, a total seven thousand years of history. Adam to Jesus was four thousand years, and in year 1999 six thousand years of human history will end. If we subtract seven years of Great Tribulation, Jesus' second coming (rapture) must take place in year 1992."[27]

One member of the sect predicted more specifically that beginning on October 28, 1992; "50 million people will die in earthquakes, 50 million in traffic accidents, 50 million from fire, 50 million from collapsed buildings, 1.4 billion from World War III and 1.4 billion from a separate Armageddon"[28]

According to press reports, as the predicted doomsday drew near, members of one sect in the northern city of Wonju burned their furniture and donned white clothing to await the Rapture.

In Seoul more than five thousand followers left their jobs. At least four suicides were reported and several abortions were performed because some women were afraid of being "too heavy" to be caught up in the air. Parents and loved ones of the movement's followers feared that if the Rapture did not take place as predicted there would be a mass suicide.

A month before October 28, Pastor Jang-Rim was arrested by Korean authorities on suspicion of embezzling church funds. Nevertheless, on October 28 about one thousand members assembled in the Tami Mission's church in Seoul to await the Rapture. Some 1,700 police officers and detectives were posted outside and inside the church in case anyone became violent or attempted suicide. Yet when the appointed hour passed uneventfully, many of the people simply wept. Said one devastated member: "God lied to us."[29]

Jang-Rim was eventually convicted of fraud and illegal possession of foreign currency. Korean authorities revealed that among his assets were bonds with maturity dates in 1995. The Tami Church was disbanded, and its leaders issued a formal apology for misleading their followers.

Also in 1999 Hon-Ming Chen and God's Salvation Church in Garland, Texas, returned with a new belief that a nuclear war would destroy parts of the earth in 1999. They identified a nine-year-old boy as the "Jesus of the East," a reincarnation of Jesus Christ. They believe that if they can link him up with the "Jesus of the West," then 100 million lives will be spared. The second Jesus was supposed to live in Vancouver, British Columbia, look like Abraham Lincoln, and have been born in late 1969. Their search still remains unsuccessful.

As the world approached the year 2000, there was a surge in the demand for end-time materials. A full quarter of Americans surveyed in a 1999 *Los Angeles Times* poll said they believe the onset of a new millennium heralds the second coming of Jesus Christ. While half of those polled said they view January 1, 2000, as just another New Year's Day, a considerable number said they expect an increase in natural disasters and civil unrest. About one in ten reported they were stockpiling goods.[30]

But Indiana State University professor Richard Pierard was not convinced all of the prognosticators were pure in their motives. About the proliferation of doomsday predictions, Pierard said, "I see this as just a bunch of nonsense and hysteria to sell books, get money, and alarm people." Pierard, an evangelical who is the coauthor of *The New Millennium Manual: A Once and Future Guide,* points the finger at Christian television and the Internet for fueling many of the chaotic Y2K predictions. "I don't see how evangelism can benefit in any way from this. It simply holds them up to ridicule," he said.

Most end-time prophecy experts would claim they rely solely on divine guidance, hours of daily research, as well as the Bible to draw their end-time scenarios. However, any world developments supporting their theories are quickly seized upon for inclusion in their papers. News about the Middle East—especially Israel—Russia, the European Common Market, smart cards, natural disasters, the Internet, and government conspiracies are fodder for the prophecy market.

Why have those armed with the best intentions and the utmost understanding of the times failed so terribly in predicting end-time events? Because the Word of God is clear on this subject of date setting. God said that neither man nor angel or even the Son of Man would know the actual date of Christ's return. That time is reserved only for God himself.

One mistake Edgar Whisenant made in his 1988 prediction was his faulty interpretation of Matthew 24:36, where Jesus speaks of his return: "But of that day and hour knoweth no man, no, not the angels of heaven, but my Father only" (KJV). Whisenant says that while we cannot know it "instinctively," with some effort we can "perceive and understand it." He even argued that while we cannot know the "day and the hour," we will know the times and the seasons—even down to the exact week.[31]

We could learn from the experience of Chuck Smith, pastor of Calvary Chapel in Costa Mesa, California. In his 1978 book *Future Survival,* Smith wrote: "From my understanding of biblical prophecies, I'm convinced that the Lord is coming for His Church before the end of 1981."

Today Smith sees the error in setting any date for things that are totally in God's hands. "Date setting is wrong, and I was guilty of coming close to that. I did believe that Hal Lindsey could have been on track when he talked about the forty-year generation, the fig tree budding being the rebirth of Israel, and I was convinced in my own heart. I never did teach it as scriptural dogma, but I had a personal conviction that Christ was coming before 1982 . . . . I've learned that we cannot put any parameters on the return—or on the rapture of the church—there are parameters—it can happen at any time, hopefully within our lifetime but maybe not."[32]

There is nothing wrong with Christians looking forward to the return of Christ. John and Paul both prayed for that day (1 Cor. 16:22; Rev. 22:20). This desire to know exactly "when and how" is as old as the first century. The disciples questioned Jesus concerning the time of the restoration of the kingdom to Israel. Jesus replied by saying: "It is not for you to know the times or the seasons, which the Father hath put in his own power" (Acts 1:6–7 KJV).

As to the second coming of the Lord, note the following Scriptures. Jesus gives clear evidence that the Christian will not know the actual date of His return:

"Watch therefore; for ye know not what hour your Lord doth come." (Matt. 24:42 KJV)

"The lord of that servant shall come in a day when he looketh not for him, and in an hour that he is not aware of." (Matt. 24:50 KJV)

"Be ye therefore ready also: for the Son of man cometh at an hour when ye think not." (Luke 12:40 KJV)

"Therefore be ye also ready: for in such an hour as ye think not the Son of man cometh." (Matt. 24:44 KJV)

"And take heed to yourselves, lest at any time your hearts be overcharged with surfeiting, and drunkenness, and cares of this life, and so that day come upon you unawares." (Luke 21:34 KJV)

"But of that day and that hour knoweth no man, no, not the angels which are in Heaven, neither the Son, but the Father." (Mark 13:32 KJV)

"Take ye heed, watch and pray: for ye know not when the time is." (Mark 13:33 KJV)

No one has ever benefited from the embarrassment and dis illusionment of failed predictions. Jesus himself said it is not for us to know the times fixed by God (Acts 1:7). But even as we pass the celebration of a new millennium, we will continue to see an acceleration in claims that Christ will come soon, and that the end is near. The fact that no one has successfully predicted the date in the past will not prevent the prognosticators from predicting or the authors from writing. What is tragic is that the potential for Christian legends could grow from the flames of men's passion to foretell the future and could ignite our curiosity regarding that which cannot be known. Author Jack Taylor says, "This is no time to worry about eschatological mysteries. Is this the terminal generation? Will Jesus come back to earth in my lifetime? How near or far are we from the end? Where does America fit into the last days? What about Israel? Iran? Iraq? Germany? Russia (what's left of it!)? What about the Antichrist?

"Read my lips: I D-O-N'-T K-N-O-W! And neither do you. The sooner we quit trying to find out what God has deemed to be none of our business the sooner we will get up to the right business."[33]

Readers beware "that ye be not soon shaken in mind, or be troubled, neither by spirit, nor by word, nor by letter as from us, as that the day Christ is at hand. Let no man deceive you by any means"(2 Thess. 2:2–3 KJV).

CHAPTER THIRTEEN

Will the Real Antichrist Please Stand Up?

→ ←

Remember the old TV quiz show *To Tell the Truth?* Three contestants appeared on stage all claiming to be the same person. Through a round of probing questions, a panel of celebrities had to determine which ones were the imposters and which contestant was telling the truth.

Imagine for a moment an episode of *To Tell the Truth* with three contenders posing as the Antichrist. Actually, you could have hundreds of imposters on that particular show because since the day of the apostle John, there have been many who could, in theory, qualify for that role. Over the last two thousand years many have been accused of being the Antichrist; however, not a single person has come forward to claim the title.

The word *antichrist* appears in just four passages in the New Testament: 1 John 2:18, 2:22, and 4:3, and 2 John 1:7. The word does not appear at all in the Book of Revelation, but the Antichrist is central to the understanding of that book. The idea of an Antichrist is also central to the apocalyptic worldview that sees human history as a struggle between God and Satan for the fate of mankind.

According to most evangelical interpretation of the books of Daniel and Revelation, the Antichrist will rise to a position of great power, promising peace to those who follow him. With the help of his own false prophet, he gains control of the world economy by forcing each person to be marked with the name of the beast or the number of its name, 666. When one of the heads of the beast appears to have a mortal wound, it is healed supernaturally, and the whole earth is filled with wonder and follows the beast. His appearance will signal the battle of Armageddon, the end of the world, and the millennial reign of Christ. Some Bible teachers believe Satan will make the Antichrist the leader of a strong European Union (similar to a revived old Roman Empire) who makes a false peace accord with Israel—only to later betray the Jewish state and make war against its people.

Some scholars believe that the "beast" described in Revelation was a coded reference to the Roman emperor Nero. The sum total of the letters in Nero's name when given their numerical equivalent in Hebrew is the number 666, described in Revelation 13:18 as the mark of the beast. Others believe that the Antichrist is not a person at all, but represents an evil society or system.

The apostle John says the spirit behind the Antichrist is already at work in the world, "and every spirit that does not confess Jesus is not from God; and this is the spirit of the antichrist, of which you have heard that it is coming, and now it is already in the world" (1 John 4:3).

He also writes, "For many deceivers have gone out into the world, those who do not acknowledge Jesus Christ as coming in the flesh. This is the deceiver and the antichrist" (2 John 7).

Despite the reality that there are two primary eschatological facts unknown to all humans—the date of the Lord's return and the identity of the Antichrist—this has never dissuaded us from trying to put a face to the name. This pursuit has been fueled with millions of dollars in seminars and in tape and book sales.

Speculation as to who really is the Antichrist has been an exercise in futility; in some cases it seems to be the only exercise some of us will ever get. Certainly the spirit of Antichrist has empowered many of the most fierce tyrants, deranged despots, and feared oppressors over the centuries, but not a one has actually stepped forward to claim the title.

In the past some in the church have painted themselves into eschatological corners when they have professed to know with certainty the exact name of the Antichrist, when he would appear, where he was from, and his role. Both distant and recent history has proven that despite all our best interpretations and projections, no one, truly, knows the Antichrist's identity.

Over the centuries many false messiahs have arisen, a sign to many that the Antichrist was near. But just when Christians thought they had their man, these counterfeit Christs did something to spoil it all—like get deposed, or worse yet, die. Here is a partial list of the many who have over the centuries either claimed to be the messiah or have had the label of Antichrist hung on them. It is by no means an exhaustive list, and I'm positive new contenders are waiting in the wings to be revealed.

ANTIOCHUS IV

Antiochus IV, also called Epiphanes ("the illustrious" or "coming one") (circa 215–164 B.C.), was the king of Syria from 175–164 B.C. During his reign he captured Jerusalem and was committed to crushing Judaism by outlawing the keeping of the Torah. So profane was Antiochus, he tried to establish the worship of Greek gods by placing an idol to Zeus inside the Holy of Holies itself. His relentless persecution of the Jews was so vile that he sacrificed a sow on the sacred altar in the temple in Jerusalem. This desecration became known as the Abomination of Desolation. Nevertheless, under the leadership of the Jewish priest Mattathias and his sons, the Maccabees, the Jews revolted and after some years drove Antiochus from Jerusalem.

On the third anniversary of the temple's desecration, the Temple was again rededicated. This rededication continues to be celebrated and is known as Hanukkah.

ROMAN EMPEROR NERO (A.D. 37–68)

Nero, the fifth emperor of Rome and the last of the Julio-Claudian line, was declared emperor at the age of seventeen. Though self-control and compassion marked the first five years of his reign, Nero had his rival, Britannicus, poisoned. In A.D. 59 he had his mother put to death for her criticism of his mistress, and in A.D. 62 he divorced and later executed his wife Octavia.

Legend has it that in July, A.D. 64, Nero fiddled while nearly two-thirds of Rome burned. He was charged with being the arsonist, but most modern scholars doubt the truth of the accusation. According to some accounts, Nero tried to lay the blame on the Christians and used the incident to persecute them. But Nero's actions caused the church to multiply even faster. When Nero learned the Roman Senate was plotting against him, he poisoned himself.

THE POPE

Since the eighth century this title has been given exclusively to the bishop of Rome, the head of the Roman Catholic Church. As the papacy gained political as well as religious power in the Middle Ages, the pope became a popular candidate for the Antichrist. The pope was a powerful leader who not only controlled the affairs of the church but held sway over kings and secular leaders by using the threat of excommunication. Once a king was barred from the church, all those who held land from a feudal lord and received protection in return for allegiance could legally take up arms against him.

Martin Luther, the German theologian who initiated the Reformation, began to think of the pope as the Antichrist mainly because of what the tradition said the Antichrist was: someone who would undermine the church from within. When he read the histories and saw the papal office subverting the gospel as he understood it, Luther became convinced that this was proof that the papal office was the office of the Antichrist.

Towards the end of his life, Luther called on his friend, painter Lucas Cranach, to create a series of woodcuts that would graphically show what Luther thought of the papacy. For example, there's one that shows the German emperor lying on the ground, and the pope standing next to him with his foot on the emperor's neck. This was intended to demonstrate Luther's belief that the papacy was trying to control secular authority throughout the world. These, Luther believed, were all actions of the Antichrist.

As an aside relating to the pope, for scholars of eschatology, one popular method of solving the mystery of the number of the beast is through the use of *gematria*. Koine Greek and biblical Hebrew do not use separate characters for numbers; so each letter in both alphabets can also represent a number.

The gematria of a word, then, is its numerical value when the letters are read as numbers and added together. For instance, "Jesus" in Greek is spelled *Ihsouß*, with the values of the letters being 10, 8, 200, 70, 400, and 200. Adding these together gives us the number 888, which is the gematria of Jesus' name. Michael Stifel, a sixteenth-century Protestant numerologist, declared that 666 was the gematria for Pope Leo X, while his Catholic contemporary Petrus Bungus insisted it stood for Martin Luther.

Many current movies and end-time books attempt to draw parallels between the Antichrist and the papacy. Rumors and wild stories of abuse, sin, and corruption have been attached to practically every pope throughout the centuries.

CHARLEMAGNE (742–814)

Charlemagne, also known as Charles the Great, was the Frankish king and Emperor of the Romans who led his armies to victory over numerous other peoples and established his rule in most of western and central Europe.

On Christmas Day A.D. 800, Charlemagne knelt to pray in Saint Peter's Basilica in Rome as Pope Leo III placed a crown upon his head, and the people assembled acclaimed him the great emperor of the Romans.

Charlemagne is renowned not only for his numerous victories but also for the size to which his empire grew as he continued to conquer lands. Many believed him to be the Antichrist because of his vision to rebuild the old Roman Empire, a task many evangelicals believed only the real Antichrist would accomplish. However, Charlemagne died before achieving his goal.

NAPOLEON (1769–1821)

Napoleon Bonaparte, the emperor of the French, institutionalized many reforms during the French Revolution. Still considered as one of the greatest military commanders of all time, Napoleon conquered a large part of Europe and did much to modernize the nations he ruled. The self-crowned French emperor did not persecute the church, and he lacked a number of the qualities needed for the role as Antichrist. His downfall was that he loved war too much. Napoleon was a driven man, never secure, never satisfied. "Power is my mistress," he said. Napoleon, like Charlemagne, worked at reviving the Roman Empire.

ALEISTER CROWLEY (1875–1947)

Between the two world wars, before the rise of Hitler, the depiction of the embodiment of evil would have been an Englishman, Aleister Crowley. To the tabloid papers of the day, he was "the King of Depravity" and "the Wickedest Man in the World." Poet W. B. Yeats spoke of Crowley as "an unspeakable degenerate," while the novelist Somerset Maugham referred to him as one of the most evil men he had ever met.

His parents were members of the Plymouth Brethren, a strict fundamentalist Christian sect. As a child, the Bible was the only book Crowley was permitted to read. Yet in time, the young Crowley rebelled against what he considered to be the bigoted atmosphere in his home. Because of his rebellion, his mother began to call him "the beast," and came to believe that her son was in fact "the Beast of the Apocalypse, the Antichrist of the Book of Revelation." It was an identity that the young Crowley happily accepted, and it set the course for the rest of his life. As a result, Aleister grew up with a thorough biblical education and an equally thorough disdain of Christianity.

While visiting Stockholm during a university vacation, Crowley decided to devote his life to the forces of evil. Crowley noted, "The forces of good were those which had constantly oppressed me. I saw them daily destroying the happiness of my fellow men. Since, therefore, it was my business to explore the spiritual world, my first step must be to get into personal communication with the devil."[1] In London, Crowley got in touch with the most influential of the occult societies operating in Britain at the time, the Hermetic Order of the Golden Dawn, an occult group that taught magic, kabala, alchemy, tarot, astrology, and other hermetic subjects. This group, like other Masonic orders, claimed to possess arcane truths handed down from ancient Egypt via the Cathars, the Knights Templar, and the Rosicrucians.

After forming his own order, Crowley, who had by now filed his canine teeth to points, staged pagan rituals with his followers, designed to bring evil spirits into their midst. The Ten Commandments were replaced by Crowley with just one: "Do what thou wilt shall be the whole of the Law." Aided by the liberal use of narcotics, the liturgies of Crowley's invention included unspeakable ritual sex acts. Today Crowley still has a following of devotees from Satanism and the Satanic Church.

ADOLF HITLER (1889–1945)

Hitler, the tyrannical German political leader who launched World War II in 1939, was one of the twentieth century's most powerful dictators. Hitler dreamed of conquering the entire world, and for a time he dominated most of Europe and North Africa. Because of his belief in a superior race, he slaughtered millions of people whom he considered inferior.

Shortly after Germany's conquest of Poland in 1939, the German army began killing thousands of Poles and driving thousands more out of their homes to make way for German occupation. The Nazis drove Jewish Poles into the city ghettoes, killing thousands of them and leaving the rest to die of starvation. Hitler also ordered a program to systematically kill all handicapped Germans, and eventually over 200,000 were murdered.

In the summer of 1941, the German authorities created a plan to kill all Jews in the portions of the USSR they occupied, but by late July, Hitler decided to extend the systematic killing of Jews to all of German-occupied Europe. After a successful German offensive in the USSR in October, Hitler decided to expand his reign of terror: all Jews everywhere would be killed. The Germans built specially designed death camps, containing large gas chambers, where Jews and other prisoners from all over could be quickly put to death by poisonous gas. Of the approximately 18 million Jews in the world, one-third were killed in what came to be known as the Holocaust. The great majority of European Jews were murdered, a fact that Hitler boasted of in his last testament.

Hitler's leadership left Germany and much of Europe in ruins. More than 60 million people died worldwide in the war, and tens of millions more lost their health and homes.

Most people would describe Hitler as the most amoral and evil man who ever lived. The spirit of Antichrist certainly inspired his campaign against the Jews and the following Holocaust. Even to this day, Hitler remains the twentieth-century model for the Antichrist.

BENITO MUSSOLINI (1883–1945)

Mussolini was the premier-dictator of Italy (the original capital of the Roman Empire) and was the founder and leader of Italian Fascism during World War II. As early as 1925, a premillennialist magazine, "Evangel," alerted their leaders to be on the lookout for the revival of the old Roman Empire. Mussolini, they warned, was "the strongest character in world politics today," and his rise to power could mean nothing other than "the climax is near." Writer Gerald Winrod's 1933 book, *Mussolini's Place n Prophecy,* concluded that all the biblical clues concerning the identity of the Antichrist pointed to Mussolini.[2] Several other Christian books and periodicals during World War II listed biblical text to prove that Hitler was the Antichrist and Mussolini was his false prophet.

KING JUAN CARLOS OF SPAIN

The late prophecy teacher Charles Taylor was a big proponent of the idea that King Juan Carlos of Spain was the Antichrist. In his newsletter, "Bible Prophecy News," dated October 1987, Taylor says, "Now a proven friend of the Jewish people and nation, King Juan Carlos is about 'ready' to become the powerful leader of the pro-Israel revived Roman Empire, and we are ready to be 'caught up' to our heavenly home! September of 1988?"[3]

King Juan Carlos is viewed as a die-hard Catholic and hereditary member of the Merovingian royal line, which claims to be descended directly from Jesus Christ and his supposed "wife," Mary Magdalene. Because of this, some end-time watchers say Juan Carlos bears careful scrutiny as a potential candidate for the position of the world's final dictator.

MAITREYA

Remember the full-page ad in the *New York Times* in 1982 proclaiming "The Christ Is Here"? Benjamin Creme, a British artist and long-time student of esoteric philosophy, was responsible for the ad about the emergence of Maitreya, the World Teacher. Throughout his early years, Creme studied various aspects of esoteric philosophy, in particular the Theosophical Society. These teachings led him to believe in the existence of the Masters of Wisdom—a group of perfected individuals who are believed to be the custodians of the Divine Plan for this planet. Creme says it came to him as a complete surprise when, in 1959, he was contacted by one of the Masters. He was told, among other things, that Maitreya, the World Teacher—the Master of all the Masters—would return in about 20 years, and that he (Creme) would have a role to play in the event, if he chose to accept it.

According to Creme, Maitreya descended in July 1977 from his ancient retreat in the Himalayas and took up residence in the Indian-Pakistani community of London. He has been living and working there, seemingly as an ordinary man, his true status known to relatively few. He has been emerging gradually into full public view so as not to infringe humanity's free will.

This New Age guru is still alive and waiting for his opportunity to save the world.

ANWAR SADAT

In her first book, *When Your Money Fails,* Mary Stewart Relfe named then-Egyptian president Anwar Sadat as "Mr. 666." Her best-selling book, published in eleven printings, established her as one of the more radical of prophecy teachers.

"After giving much time to studying the scriptural qualifications, characteristics, and prerequisites, my prudent assessment is that President Anwar Sadat of Egypt is either history's nearest prototype or the real 'Mr. 666'," she wrote.[4] Sadly, Sadat was assassinated in 1981.

JIMMY CARTER

Prophecy teacher Doug Clark, host of "Shockwaves of Armageddon," announced in 1976 that President Jimmy Carter would be "the president who will meet Mr. 666 (the Antichrist) soon!" As late as June 1983, prophecy teacher James McKeever reprinted in *End Times News Digest* an article that questioned the activities of the former president in Israel. According to the article, Carter was really in Israel to prepare for the unveiling of the Antichrist.[5]

RONALD WILSON REAGAN

During the 1980s, while Reagan was president of the United States, there was a belief by some that he could be the Antichrist because all three of his names were made up of six letters each. Some overzealous Christians thought the near-death shooting of Regan's press secretary, James Brady, could be a prophetic sign. If Brady is seen as one of the heads of our government, then the attack on his life could have been the fulfillment of Revelation 13:3: "One of the heads of the beast seemed to have had a fatal wound, but the fatal wound had been healed. The whole world was astonished and followed the beast" (NIV).

MIKHAIL GORBACHEV

As the first Russian leader to support rights for the people of the Soviet Union and a staunch proponent of one world government, Gorbachev still remains a candidate for the job of Antichrist in the minds of fervent Antichrist watchers. Once again, Charles Taylor claimed that Gorby's name stood for Gog—a name commonly identified as the Soviet Union—thought to invade Israel according to Ezekiel 37 and 38. In 1988 Taylor wrote in his newsletter, "With the Moslems ready to declare all-out holy war (Jihad) and with GOGrbachev (Russian spelling for Gorbachev) in a much greater power position today and King Juan Carlos of Spain taking his proper position as the next chairman of the Common Market on January 1, 1989, all the loose ends seem to be coming to climax."[6]

For most of the twentieth century the Soviet Union was associated with communism, socialism, and atheism. Many Americans were worried about the rhetoric coming from Soviet leaders, fearing an all-out war between the U.S. and "The Evil Empire"—

especially after advances in the late 1950s space race and the Cuban missile crisis.

Gorbachev was the general secretary of the Communist Party from 1985 to 1991 and president of the Soviet Union in 1990–91. His efforts to democratize his country's political system and decentralize its economy led to the downfall of communism and the breakup of the Soviet Union in 1991. Gorbachev resigned as head of the communist party on August 24, 1991, and as president on December 25, 1991. After his resignation, the USSR and the Iron Curtain dissolved. Despite the fact Gorbachev is well liked outside of the Russian borders, he was unsuccessful in his bid for the presidency in 1996.

Today, Gorbachev has become one of the world's foremost speakers emphasizing the need for a new world order and a strengthened United Nations, without any country having the power of veto. Besides being president of Green Cross International, he is founder of the Gorbachev Foundation. It sponsored a "State of the World" forum and brought together hundreds of world leaders and corporate heads, including astronomer Carl Sagan, media mogul Ted Turner, former President George Bush, and former British Prime Minister Margaret Thatcher.

Some Christians are suspect of anyone with ties to "godless communism," the U.N., a new world order, large corporations, and powerful world leaders. In Gorby's case, he's got it all. And if that's not enough, some are trying to make too much of that birthmark on his head, thinking it to somehow be "the mark of the beast."

SADDAM HUSSEIN

Even before the Gulf War, Saddam was looked on by some as the "beast" of Daniel and Revelation. Shortly after taking office as president of Iraq, Hussein purged and murdered dozens of government officials suspected of disloyalty. In the early 1980s, he used chemical weapons to crush a Kurdish rebellion in northern Iraq. Bent on dominating the Muslim world, he attacked neighboring countries, and in 1980 invaded Iran, launching an eight-year war that ended in stalemate.

Saddam is seldom seen in public in Iraq; yet his presence is felt ever there, looking down from gigantic posters depicting him as a mythical hero.

SUN MYUNG MOON

On August 24, 1992, at a gathering of one thousand world leaders at the World Culture and Sports Festival, Reverend Moon declared that he and his wife are the Messiah and True Parents of all humanity. In her speech before the group, Mrs. Moon gave this explanation: "Ladies and Gentlemen, what is the Messiah? The Messiah is the True Parents of humankind. God's original plan was to establish perfected Adam and Eve as the true ancestors of humanity. Satan, however, invaded this ideal, and God, ever since, has been working toward the emergence of ideal True Parents through which all humankind can be restored. As true fathers and true mothers ourselves, we must vanquish Satan, liberate humanity and build the kingdom of Heaven on earth. As God's sons and daughters, we must inherit God's love, life and lineage. Moreover, we must also inherit True Parents' love, life and lineage. Then we will have achieved unity between heaven and earth, vertical and horizontal, and mind and body. This will be the starting point for the eternal world of peace."[7]

According to the Unification Church's biography of Rev. Moon, on Easter in 1935, Jesus appeared to him as he was praying in the Korean mountains. In that vision, Jesus asked him to continue the work that he had begun on earth nearly 2,000 years before. Jesus asked him to complete the task of establishing God's kingdom on earth and bringing his peace to humankind.

Nevertheless, Moons' own life has been troubled. A five-year IRS investigation produced an indictment against Reverend Moon. Handed down in 1981, Moon was charged with evading income taxes nearly a decade earlier, as well as conspiracy to avoid those taxes. Moon spent thirteen months in Danbury Federal Prison.

LOUIS FARRAKHAN

Farrakhan is known for having called the Jewish faith "a gutter religion," and referring to German dictator Adolf Hitler, who was responsible for killing millions of Jews, as a great man. Farrakhan has been promoting the teachings of the late Elijah Muhammad (founder of the Nation of Islam in the 1930s) for more than forty years. "Minister Farrakhan," the preferred term to designate the leader of the revived Nation of Islam, has twice been on the cover of *Time* magazine and has been the featured subject for hundreds of newspaper and magazine articles worldwide.

Despite such a public profile, Farrakhan's controversial remarks at press conferences have been widely condemned by other black leaders. The growth of the Nation of Islam has caused concern because its doctrines challenge the Christian truth on every major front: the nature of God, the validity of the Bible, the person and work of Christ, and the idea of life after death. Farrakhan has said that Jesus was "just a prophet" and he, Louis Farrakhan, is the true Jesus.

BILL GATES, FOUNDER OF MICROSOFT

An e-mail warning sent in the late 1990s reveals Bill Gates as the Antichrist. But the conclusions one must draw from this are further proof that this e-mail message is a hoax. Here is a reproduction of the message I received some time ago:

Subject: Bill Gates

Did you know that Bill Gates' real name is
William Henry Gates III?
Nowadays, he is known as Bill Gates (III)
where III means the order of third. So what's so
eerie about this name? Well, if you take all the let-
ters in Bill Gates III and then convert it into
ASCII code (American Standard Code for
Information Interchange) and then add up all the

numbers. . . . you will get 666, which is the number of the beast.

B = 66
I = 73
L = 76
L = 76
G = 71
A = 65
T = 84
E = 69
S = 83
I = 1
I = 1
I = 1

Add these numbers and they equal 666.

Coincidence? Perhaps. . . . Maybe, but take Windows 95 and do the same procedure and you will get 666 also. And even MS-DOS 6.31 adds up to 666. Still think it is coincidence?

Would it be too surprising if Bill Gates was the antichrist? After all, the Bible foretells that someone powerful would rise up and lead the world to destruction. And Bill Gates definitely has this kind of power in his hands. More than 80% of computers in the world today run on Windows and DOS (including those at the Pentagon). If all of his products have some kind of small program embedded, like this "hall of tortured souls," that can give him control to set off nuclear arsenals, create havoc in security systems and financial systems all over the world, etc., all from his headquarters. This isn't too far from reality. Just by using the Internet Explorer you may allow him to map out what you have on your computer bit by bit each time you log on.

Perhaps the end of time is near and this is just a tip of the iceberg?

Here is something to ponder. Isn't everything going towards the Internet? (i.e., buying, selling, business transactions). Isn't Microsoft always on the move to have a monopoly when it comes to software technology? And now the Internet? Revelation also says that the mark of the beast will be carved on one's hand and on one's forehead. If the Internet would indeed be the beast, aren't we all starting to carry it on our hands and foreheads? The computer screen is our forehead and our hand is attached to the mouse. Is it that big of a stretch? Are things finally starting to fall into place or are we just letting our imaginations run???? Remember, the devil came to cheat, steal and to destroy. So, be vigilant about Bill Gates and Microsoft!

Coincidence? Perhaps.

To answer the question in this message "is it too big of a stretch to believe?" Yes! To suggest Bill Gates or anyone for that matter has the time to read the contents of millions of computers is unreasonable. I guess this means only Apple computer users are safe from the coming wrath of Bill the Antichrist.

PRINCE CHARLES OF WALES

According to the book *Antichrist and a Cup of Tea* by Tim Cohen and research by prophecy teachers Jim Searcy and Monte Judah, Prince Charles, unlike all previous candidates, has many qualifications deemed necessary to be the Antichrist. They claim his name calculates to 666 in both English and Hebrew, the symbols in his heraldic coat of arms are identical to those of the "first beast" of Revelation 13, and he reportedly claims descent from David, Jesus, and Mohammed. One teacher claims Charles has a traceable biochip implant, while another end-time lecturer proclaimed that Charles was to have ascended the Temple Mount in Jerusalem in March of 1998 and proclaim himself the Christ. He obviously didn't.

The royal spin-doctors may want to work on his approval rating in his own country before trying to get most of the world to follow him.

BARNEY THE DINOSAUR

From the ridiculous to the sublime, proof that Barney the dinosaur is the Antichrist has appeared many places on the Internet. Here's the proof: The Romans had no letter U and used V instead for printing, so the Roman representation for Barney would be:

CVTE PVRPLE DINOSAVR

Extracting the Roman numerals, we have C - V - V - L - D - I - V

And their decimal equivalents are 100 - 5 - 5 - 50 - 500 - 1 - 5

Adding those numbers produces 666. This is the number of the beast.

Therefore Barney is the Antichrist.

Others who have been accused over the years of being the Antichrist by various prophecy buffs include Henry Kissinger; the late Pope Paul VI; Karl Von Hapsburg, heir to the Hapsburg Austrian throne; Libyan leader Muammar Qadhafi; and Christian broadcaster Pat Robertson. Not a single one has stepped forward to claim the crown.

History seems to indicate that our pursuit to pin-the-tale-on-the-Antichrist has rarely led Christians to much productivity. This inexorable obsession appears to have done more to forestall than expand the Kingdom of God on earth.

Prophecy teachers commonly claim that their research was painstakingly done, with numerous sources, and a biblical basis. Yet in their desire to be the one to uncover the Antichrist, they have brought God's Word into disrepute through their inaccurate predictions. Rather than bringing men and women to salvation, they are aiding in the confusion that will mark the last days. "Know this first of all, that in the last days mockers will come with their mocking, following after their own lusts, and saying, 'Where is the promise of His coming? For ever since the fathers fell asleep, all continues just as it was from the beginning of creation'" (2 Pet. 3:3–4).

Prophecy teacher David Lewis confesses, "The tragedy is that the message [of prophecy] has been attacked by its enemies, eroded by its friends, and ignored by everybody else."[8]

Many have relied on astrology, numerology, mathematical calculations, and questionable sources to come up with their conclusions. Could it be that their misrepresentation of the truth may actually play into the hands of the real Antichrist? With years of crying "wolf," will the body of Christ even notice when the real man of sin is revealed?

While most Bible prophecy is open to many interpretations, and some have recklessly mishandled it, the serious study of prophecy should be handled with care. Discernment and wisdom are needed as well as a caution against a rush to judgment. True Bible prophecy should build our faith, not cause us to go into hiding whenever trouble flares up in the world. Prophecy is a message of hope, not hype. The message to the church at Sardis in Revelation is, "Because you have kept the word of My perseverance, I also will keep you from the hour of testing, that [hour] which is about to come upon the whole world, to test those who dwell upon the earth. I am coming quickly; hold fast what you have, in order that no one take your crown" (Rev. 3:10–11).

This is an hour to stay alert, contend for our faith, and go boldly into the entire world with the life-changing message of our Lord. An obsessive desire to prove who is the Antichrist, and exactly when he will appear, has only led to confusion, divisiveness, and unwarranted fear. But it has sold a lot of tapes.

CHAPTER FOURTEEN

Y2K—The Bug
That Didn't Bite

➔ ❖ ❖

Will all the world's computers shut down? Will the lights go off? Will I need to stockpile food and water? These were some of the basic questions—and fears—people had about Y2K. While no one knew for sure what would happen on New Year's Day 2000, the setting was ripe for many myths to be tied to a potentially serious problem.

Let's remind ourselves exactly what the Y2K bug was all about. "Y2K" was an abbreviation for the year 2000 and essentially became the label for any series of computer glitches that were predicted to cause serious breakdowns on January 1, 2000.

Large sectors of society and a global economy would be vulnerable to disruption if the world's computers were unable to recognize the year 2000, mistaking it for 1900.

The root of the problem dates back to 1960 when the computer language COBOL, Common Business Oriented Language, was developed by a team drawn from the Pentagon and several computer manufacturers. As the programmers started writing the computer code, they used six digits for dates—two digits each for the month, day, and year—to save costly computer memory space. For example, June 14, 1998, would be represented as "061498." Software programs could have read the year "00," as 1900. Even then, computer scientists, anticipating problems, urged companies to use the four-digit year as problems were expected when dates in the year 2000 were entered.

While large corporations and the federal government worked hard to fix the Y2K bug in their computer systems, by the end of 1998 several institutions vital to American life had not. Experts held conflicting views as to the extent of the problems that could result if a fix could not be found for the Y2K bug. Some of the potential disastrous scenarios were:

- A hospital's computer could fail while attempting to trace a patient's prescription and medical records. The information about a prescription's expiration date could indicate that the medication is already expired, preventing prescription refills.
- The 911 emergency system phone grid could malfunction, leaving the city's population at risk for slow response by emergency personnel.
- Residents could lose access to local public services such as heat, light, water, sewage, telephone, police, medical services, and transportation. These power failures might endanger the elderly, ill, or infirm.
- The police may not be able to trace the records of known criminals, or their fingerprints, and jails could mistakenly release the wrong prisoners.

- Plant operators may not be able to access the remote shut-down if security computers in nuclear plants [lock and fail safe] because of Y2K rollover problems.

In early 1998, discussions of anticipated Y2K computer problems were primarily held among computer programmers and network security experts. But by year's end, every major news outlet had created a public awareness to the potential threat. "In terms of maturity, we've gone from a bland awareness that it might be a problem to an enormous focus in late summer and early fall on survivalists. I see that moving into community awareness," said Ed Yourdon, author of more than two dozen books on software engineering.[1]

COMMENTS FROM GOVERNMENT OFFICIALS

In April 1999 the chairman of the Senate Y2K committee took to the Sunday morning talk shows to warn that a little stockpiling of food and water never hurt.[2] By the summer of 1999, Arnaud deBorchgrave, the president of the Center for Strategic and International Studies, compared Y2K to "a series of electronic tornadoes zapping the world in crazy quilt patterns. [It's] [i]mpossible to predict who's going to get hurt and who is going to emerge unscathed. Obviously, many people are going to emerge unscathed and many organizations—countries—will be damaged and damaged severely, especially in the developing world."[3]

One of the biggest worries for most people was the nation's infrastructure —utilities like power and water. Senator Robert Bennett, the chairman of the U.S. Senate Special Committee on the Year 2000 Technology Problem, felt positive that most of the nation was prepared. "In the United States, many, if not most, will go through the year 2000 without knowing it, without noticing it. The basic infrastructure issues now are pretty much under control," Bennett said.[4]

But while that was good news to many, in August 1999, National Association of State Information Resource Executives data showed only three states—Iowa, Nebraska, and North

Dakota—had completed Y2K fixes to their "mission critical" systems. However, Jack Gribben, spokesperson for the President's Council on Year 2000, said there was cause for cautious optimism: "I think it is clear that a number of states still have work left to do on critical systems, [but] a substantial number of states are more than 75 percent done with implementation work."[5] Amazingly, as late as mid-December 1999, Alabama reported that the state government had 328 critical computer systems, with 57 percent of them compliant with Y2K. The next worst state, New Mexico, reported that 81 percent of its critical computer systems were Y2K compliant.

Many had fears that due to the Y2K bug, our military would be ill equipped to handle any urgent situation both here and abroad. In preparation for Y2K, the Pentagon spent $3.6 billion fixing Defense Department computers to deal with the start of the year 2000. "I think you can anticipate there are going to be some problems with computer systems abroad," John Hamre, the deputy defense secretary, told reporters in a December 1999 briefing on the Pentagon's Y2K preparations. Asked if he thought there was any likelihood that the problems could lead to military hostilities, Hamre said, "I think we're going to be fine."[6] Of the 2,101 computer systems deemed critical to the department's war fighting mission, only two were deemed not ready.

In what was considered a dress rehearsal of what some computer programmers considered things to come, September 9, 1999, or 9-9-99 went off without a hitch. Experts were afraid computers would confuse the date of four nines with an "end-program" command. Early computer programmers often used the numerical notation for September 9, 1999, as the date representing infinity. They were sure the databases or programs would be replaced long before the actual day rolled around.

Inadequate Y2K preparations were much more worrisome overseas, particularly in China, Russia, Italy, and several countries the United States depends on for oil. Some worried the threat of serious breakdowns could rattle the global economy. With Russia behind in Y2K compliance and armed nuclear missiles still sitting at the ready in both countries, a center was established in Colorado to jointly monitor launch data. A modified data feed designed to protect national security pumped information into a specially-created work area, where American and Russian operators worked together till mid-January 2000 to watch for any unexpected launches that might be related to Y2K glitches.

In a move supported by the British government's Action 2000, the administration of Prime Minister Tony Blair sent a twenty-four-page Y2K brochure to all 26 million homes in the UK. The intent of the mailer was to calm the fears of British citizens, and urge them not to stockpile food, water, currency, and other basic supplies.

The U.S. Senate Special Committee on the Year 2000 Technology Problem concluded that claims of problems overseas might be greatly inflated. The report predicted, "Severe long- and short-term disruptions to supply chains are likely to occur. Such disruptions may cause a low to moderate downturn in the economy, particularly in those industries that depend upon foreign supplies." Nevertheless, the panel took pains to avoid inflaming undue alarm, warning that "sensationalists" who "fuel rumors of massive Y2K failures and government conspiracies" are off-base.[7]

Still, the U.S. House of Representatives' last Y2K hearing in November 1999 reflected little of the doom, gloom, and tedium that marked early sessions, and focused mainly on Y2K myths and realities. Presidential advisor John A. Koskinen said the consensus was that the power grid, the phone system, and the banks would operate normally come January 1, 2000. But Koskinen also offered, "One of the more troubling Y2K myths is the notion that January 1 is a seminal date which everything, or nothing, Y2K-related will occur."

"Whatever people are going to do to prepare, they should do it early," he said. "If everyone waits until the last moment to take even modest precautions, supply systems could be overwhelmed."[8]

WHAT COMPUTER EXPERTS SAY

Despite restrained reports from the government sector, some computer and software experts feared a catastrophic end because of the Y2K bug. Cory Hamasaki, a systems programmer and computer consultant with twenty-nine years of experience, warned of the extinction of the human race in his November 1998 newsletter. Hamasaki wrote, "We must also prepare ourselves for the very real possibility that the outcome of this situation might well be the total extinction of the entire human race. It really could be worse than I am predicting and I really am being optimistic. First, I would like to assure you that I am not some kind of nut anxiously waiting for the end of the world. . . ."

He goes on to say, "I have been studying Y2K in every way possible to me since October of 1997. On a daily basis. How many hours? I don't want to know. In that time I have become convinced that we are going to get blasted. Big time blasted. Info magic blasted. I have learned enough to get real —— scared, scared motionless like a rabbit facing a snake."

In his January 1998 newsletter, Hamasaki also wrote, "[You should cache] most of your arms and supplies, while this is still possible and legal. Preferably, you should have several smaller caches known only to you and to a highly trusted backup . . . someone who will pass the supplies on to your family or group if anything happens to you. . . . You need to convert most of your spare cash and paper investments into gold and/or silver coins."[9]

Consultant Bruce Webster predicted an economic crisis in his book *The Y2K Survival Guide*. Webster warned of "Economic slowdown . . . unemployment rises . . . interruptions in utilities . . . common use of heaters, cook stoves . . . increase in layoffs . . . some neighborhoods forming purchasing associations . . . . [Probability of this outcome or worse] is 65 percent."[10]

WHAT CHRISTIANS SAY

Like the computer experts, Christian conservatives were divided on the Y2K issue. Countless radio and television programs, Web sites, and books warned believers to prepare for the widespread public collapse predicted to follow the crash of millions of critical services infected with the so-called Y2K bug. Some of doomsayers predicted the millennium bug would spark the end of modern society, as we know it. The stock market would crash, banks would close as everybody simultaneously withdrew their money, people would riot in the streets when they didn't get their government checks, the energy and transportation infrastructures would collapse, and chaos would rule.

In early 1997 author Gary North wrote about the coming Y2K disaster from his Web site *garynorth.com:* "The problem will not be fixed. Everyone in authority will deny that time has run out to get this fixed, right up until December 31, 1999, . . . I'm saying that it's over. Right now. It cannot be fixed. Whatever it does, the Millennium Bug will bite us."[11]

In October 1999 North added, "I maintain that the Y2K problem is systemic. It cannot be fixed. The interconnections are too many. A noncompliant computer will spread bad data and re-corrupt a compliant computer. They cannot all be fixed. There is no agreed-upon standard for even the placement of the century date. Either the noncompliant computers will recorrupt the compliant ones, or the compliant ones must cease all contact with noncompliant ones, thereby shutting down entire systems, most notably the banking system. If we can't fix almost all noncompliant computers (and we can't), it does no permanent good to fix any of them. This is the 'dirty little secret' of the computer-programming guild."[12]

High-profile leaders gave impetus to the fears by voicing their own concerns and linking them to apocalyptic prophecies in the New Testament's Book of Revelation.[13] The Southwest Radio Church, a nondenominational prophetic ministry, sounded the doomsday warning bell by suggesting: "When the world information systems fail on a massive level on January 1, 2000, it will necessitate involuntary compliance with a whole new information system. . . . Is this the event which will prove to be the harbinger of the mark of the beast system?"[14]

A book Ed Yourdon coauthored with his daughter Jennifer, *Time Bomb 2000,* hit the bookstores in January 1998 and remained on the *New York Times'* business best-seller list for five months. Yourdon expected numerous deaths from hypothermia and starvation. "It won't be the end of civilization, but the year 2000 problem could trigger a depression on the scale of the Great Depression in the U.S. during the 1930s."[15]

But by the end of 1998, the Yourdons were no longer alone in preaching Y2K awareness. There were plenty of books on the subject of Y2K, among them titles like *Y2K Chaos* and *Y2K 2000: Worldwide Collapse.* Popular prophecy teacher Grant Jeffrey's book, *The Millennium Meltdown,* explored the potential of the year 2000 computer meltdown setting the stage for the rise of the world government of the Antichrist.

Another best-seller, *The Millennium Bug—How to Survive the Coming Chaos,* by author Michael S. Hyatt, articulated what could happen when the year 2000 arrived—power grids going dark, 911 call centers unavailable, widespread starvation, and the industrialized world reduced to chaos. The book uses lots of quotes and case studies, news items, and endnote references to the author's sources. Written to help prepare for a worst-case scenario, Hyatt's advice included moving to small towns, stockpiling food and water, and arming yourself to fend off any looters. Though Hyatt claimed he was not an expert, he was proud of that fact because "it was the experts who got us into this mess."[16]

Hyatt warned, "We've got a digital hurricane coming that's got the potential for simultaneous, multiple disruptions. While I am stubbornly optimistic that it will be between a brownout and a blackout, I am more pessimistic today than I was. That this hasn't been raised to a national emergency is amazing."[17]

In his novel about what happens in the year 2000 when the world's computers malfunction, *Y2K: The Day the World Shut Down,* Hyatt and coauthor George Grant predicted a stock market crash. In the fictional story of Bob Priam, husband, father of three, and Chief Information Officer of a Fortune 500 company, conflict arises as he desperately tries to alert his CEO to the potential danger of the Y2K bug. An excerpt from the book describes the tension Bob Priam feels as his world crashes around him: "The stock market crashed and there was a run on the banks. . . . We've been only too aware that the fractional reserve banking system was unwise and insecure. . . . The safest place in the whole universe right now is not in the center of the securest compound money can buy. It is in the center of God's will."[18]

Shaunti Christine Feldhahn, a former Federal Reserve Board analyst, wrote *Y2K: The Millennium Bug,* which recommended, among other things, that churches and individuals stockpile food in anticipation of major computer-related breakdowns. Feldhahn founded the nonprofit organization Joseph Project 2000 to inform churches and pastors about the computer bug. The inspiration for the group's name came from the Old Testament story of Joseph, who was sold into Egyptian slavery only to rise to become a prince and save the country from a coming famine by planning ahead.

HOW WE RESPONDED

The anxiety and uncertainty in the hearts of American Christians increasingly grew as they struggled to discern what the truth was about Y2K. In a two-part series on Y2K featured in *Religion Today,* editors quoted Jim Jacobson, president of Christian Freedom International, as saying, "One congregation ousted its pastor because he was 'not diehard enough' about preparing for Y2K. Another church nearly went through a split because of a disagreement over the issue." Larry Pierce, one of the editors, stated he knew members of his church that have already moved in preparation of the upcoming Y2K disaster.[19]

Afraid that the Y2K computer crash would cause power outages and anarchy, Bob Rutz and his wife left their home in California to build a Christian community called Prayer Lake in the Ozark Mountains of Arkansas. "I look at it as Judgment Day," said Rutz, a sixty-six-year old engineer. "Instead of putting up the barricades and piling up the bodies, we've got to minister to those hurting people down the road."[20] The Rutzes hoped to take one hundred families with them when they moved.

Concerns about Y2K also helped persuade Jerry and Carolyn Head to move from a Dallas suburb to an eighty-five-acre farm near Harrison, Arkansas. Jerry doesn't see himself like most survivalists. "Most of them are nuts," he said. Carolyn agrees. "We're planners," she explained. Planning for them meant buying a home generator, a one-thousand-gallon propane tank, and a small flock of chickens. The Head's son, David, seemed confident when he said, "God's going to protect us. But we're also preparing. I'm not afraid of hard work." Their daughter Sarah, who was preparing for college in the fall, expected to be home in the winter. "I don't want to be away when something happens," she said. The Heads expected cash to be of no value after Y2K, so they stashed hundreds of rolls of toilet paper throughout their four-bedroom house. "These are good barter items," Jerry explained.[21]

Harrison, Arkansas, a quiet Ozarks Mountain town of eleven thousand, was fast becoming a mecca for anyone who feared the worst. Up to one hundred of the locals attended twice-monthly meetings of a group called Y2K Watch. In August 1998, a Y2K meeting brought at least seven hundred people to an auditorium at North Arkansas College. The organizer of the meeting, former town mayor Dan Harness, gathered representatives from a local utility, bank, hospital, and phone company. "My purpose was not to scare anyone but to begin talking about economic self-sufficiency."[22]

Y2K MERCHANDISERS

There was also a significant increase in the purchase of survivalists' gear, freeze-dried foods, and generators in the months leading up to January 1, 2000. Steve Portela, manager of Walton Feed in

Montpelier, Idaho, one of the largest sellers of freeze-dried and dehydrated foods, reported, "Orders are backing up." The bulk of his customers for emergency food traditionally have been his fellow Mormons, whose religion calls on them to set aside a year's supply of food. But with the concern about Y2K, he had seen a dramatic increase in the number of non-Mormon customers.[23]

Preparedness Resources Inc., a twenty-year-old Utah purveyor of dehydrated foods, saw monthly sales zoom from $300,000 in December 1977 to $4 million in November 1998. "Y2K is driving the worry," said office manager Roslyn Niebuhr.[24] Like Walton Feed, until 1995 the company did most of its business with Mormons, but by 1998, as much as 90 percent of sales have been to non-Mormons.

Marvin Tarlton and his neighbors in Marshville, North Carolina, a rural community thirty miles southeast of Charlotte, stocked his farm pond with fish, bought bags of dried pinto beans, and kept six hundred canning jars on hand to preserve vegetables they may have to grow.

"We're preparing a little more radical than others," said Tarlton, 39. "I feel good, but I'm not where I want be."[25] Like others who stored provisions just in case, Tarlton cites Proverbs 27:12: "The prudent see danger and take refuge, but the simple keep going and suffer for it" (NIV).

CHRISTIAN MODERATES

Some Christians held a more moderate position and maintained that vital systems would be ready. They admitted that the Y2K bug was a real problem, and it needed to be fixed, but they held that those who were actually working on the millennium bug did not expect anything near the apocalyptic scenarios put forth by the doomsayers.

Steve Hewitt, founder and editor-in-chief of *Christian Computing*® magazine said he was amazed at how much emotion was involved while discussing the subject of Y2K. He believed while it started as a computer bug, the conversations soon became entrenched in politics and religion. Those who believed the world would have a real disaster did not want to tolerate those who disagreed.

Hewitt wrote in one article, "If you do not agree with those making the rounds among our churches preaching that Y2K will be a disaster, you will be accused of being in 'denial.' Of course, no one wants to be in denial. The very term implies you have something wrong with you psychologically. However, such attacks fail to take into account that some of us have studied the data and just happen to disagree with their assessment."[26]

"Christians are not called to fear, but to trust in God," Hewitt added. "Yes, we are to live in wisdom and not act as fools, but I do not believe we are to live our lives expecting a 'worst case scenario.'"[27]

My friend Jim Hylton, the pastor of MetroChurch in Edmond, Oklahoma, called for reason and calm in a two-part series "How to Face a Threatening Bug." In this excerpt from that sermon, Jim reassured the church about the various myths of Y2K:

> It will be more than a bump in the road, I believe. But it will not approach the pileup of cars that occurs after hitting a band of fog on a busy California freeway. I believe it will be more like cars going into an intersection where the traffic lights have gone out. There will be some fender-benders and some horn honking, resulting in considerable delays and inconveniences.
>
> We can have a positive reaction to these potential problems as Christians. There is no reason to become a doomsayer. God's Word gives us instructions about how to face adversity, the purpose of the adversity, and the supply of wisdom that God offers. . . .
>
> This week I called my friend in San Diego, Larry Goshorn, who builds robots and satellites

using the latest computer technology. Again I asked for his assessment from a technical aspect in regards to Y2K. All of his information and conversations with people who have advanced computer knowledge leads him to be optimistic that the problem we face is not cataclysmic. He has concern that the people who are "crying wolf," when only the neighbor's dog is approaching, have raised false fears and, in some instances, are exploiting those fears by their fees to speak and sell information. He is a person who hears from the Lord and has heard nothing about pending doom brought on by failed technology.

So as Christians, we need to see an opportunity for prayer and claiming victory from the Lord as our greatest hope. We must not buy into a faithless approach to Y2K. It is not time for panic but for prayer and preparation in our hearts. We can speak a positive word regarding this issue. There are some steps of a practical nature that need to be taken.

"For the Lord is watching his children, listening to their prayers; but the Lord's face is hard against those who do evil. Usually no one will hurt you for wanting to do good. But even if they should, you are to be envied, for God will reward you for it. Quietly trust yourself to Christ your Lord, and if anybody asks why you believe as you do, be ready to tell him, and do it in a gentle and respectful way. Do what is right; then if men speak against you, calling you evil names, they will become ashamed of themselves for falsely accusing you when you have only done what is good. Remember, if God wants you to suffer, it is better to suffer for doing good than for doing wrong!

Christ also suffered. He died once for the sins of
all us guilty sinners, although he himself was innocent of any sin at any time, that he might bring us
safely home to God. But though his body died,
his spirit lived on" (1 Pet. 3:12–18 TLB).

There was, however, a distinct backlash among others within
the conservative Christian community against many of those who
painted disastrous scenarios. Among the more aggressive, Hank
Hanegraaff, host of the popular *Bible Answer Man* radio show,
spent hour after on-air hour debunking Y2K warnings and casti-
gating those he considers responsible. In an interview, he said
"Many (sic) influential conservative Christians had been taken in
by 'profiteering sensationalists' spreading 'alarmist propaganda,'
even if they have since changed their tune."[28]

Charisma, the respected monthly charismatic-oriented magazine, ran a cover story in July 1999 headlined "Doomsday
Madness." The cover depicted a terrified family huddled in a
basement filled with packaged foods and barrels of water. In one
hand the father held a flashlight, in the other, he clutched a Bible.
Inside the magazine, editor J. Lee Grady dismissed most of the
Y2K warnings as nonsense.

Many Christian organizations studied the Y2K issue and
developed thoughtful responses. A three-day *Focus on the Family*
radio series hosted by James Dobson drew a very receptive audience. "There is a middle ground between panicking and doing
nothing, and that's what we're trying to find," Dobson said.[29]
Major denominations, including Episcopal, Roman Catholic,
United Methodist, Presbyterian, Southern Baptist, and
Pentecostals, worked for months to put their computer systems in
order by the end of 1999. The Assemblies of God reported they
worked five years on resolving Y2K. The General Council in
Springfield, Missouri, warned members against "needless fear and
alarmists tactics," such as hoarding food and believing doomsday
scenarios that conflict with the Lord's teachings.

"We have the message of hope from our Lord who has taught us to fear not. Rather than fearing the collapse of computers or society, the Scriptures call upon us to fear God's wrath. The good news is that God's wrath need never be experienced when we place our trust in Jesus as Savior and Lord."[30]

Presiding Bishop H. George Anderson of the Evangelical Lutheran Church in America issued a pastoral letter warning people to dismiss "wild prophecies." Urging calm to counter speculation and fear, Anderson said, "We expect more craziness as we get closer to the event."[31]

There were even optimistic voices among government officials. Sally Katzen, the director of the Office of Management and Budget, had overseen more than twenty-four federal agencies. As early as 1997 she said, "We have a high degree of confidence that the important services and benefits will continue through and after the new millennium. It is my expectation that when we wake up on January 1 in the year 2000, the millennium bug will have been a nonevent."

So confident that air traffic wouldn't be affected, Rodney Slater, U.S. secretary of Transportation, along with John Koskinen, assistant to the president and chair of the President's Council on Year 2000 Conversion, and Jane Garvey, Federal Aviation Administration administrator, planned to fly from New York to San Francisco on December 31, 1999. The flight was in the air during the 7:00 P.M. eastern standard time, New Year's rollover time for the air traffic control system, which operates on Greenwich Mean Time. The flight took off and arrived on time and was without incident.

Financial institutions like Chase Manhattan, Norwest, and KeyCorp had already begun fixing their bad code even before 1998 was over. The electrical power industry said it had completed most of its Y2K compliance work. In all likelihood, there would be no major disruptions in most places. What was uncertain at the time was how localized the breakdowns could be and how quick the response to them would be if and when they did happen. Engineers working on home appliances and computers also predicted few if any problems because of the dreaded embedded chip.

So, when clocks finally rolled over to mark the year 2000, even the most optimistic forecasts were too grim. The computer catastrophe that seemed so terrible was a flop. Even nations like Russia, China, India, and others seen as vulnerable reported no significant Y2K glitches. In Paraguay, for instance, where the government waited until mid-1999 to start addressing the Y2K problem, the country's Y2K coordinator reported all basic services, including electricity, telephones, and water, were functioning normally on New Year's Day.

There was so little news coming from our government's Y2K command center on New Year's Eve that some television techs popped in a video—*Apocalypse Now*. The first business day of 2000 began with abundant energy supplies and corporate computer systems working smoothly.

REFLECTIONS

So why was the Y2K bug apparently all bark and no byte?

Technology analysts credit the unusual cooperation among businesses and governments worldwide, as well as the mobilization of people as possible answers. But some wondered aloud whether some of their previous assumptions had been wrong all along. No one disputed it was a real problem that needed to be fixed, but most organizations representing vital services expected to be ready all along.

While some computer-related, and not necessarily Y2K-related, glitches did hit, the Y2K bug was not to be found. A report from the Senate Special Committee on the Year 2000 Technology Problem listed minor Y2K problems in the U.S., including Medicare payment delays, double-billing by some credit card companies, degradation of a spy satellite system, a few ATM machines reportedly shut down, 911 problems in several localities, and a nuclear weapons plant system "anomaly." Since the beginning of the year 2000, there have been mostly isolated reports of malfunctions, but no reports of the devastating failures some feared.

Yet even as most of our worst fears were being calmed, there were those who stuck to their guns, so to speak. Steve Heller, a computer programmer and author, fled to rural east Texas and spent $100,000 on Y2K systems and supplies, including a steam engine. "The one thing I didn't expect was that nothing would happen, but I acted rationally on the information I had," he asserts.[32]

Books that once boldly predicted a Y2K apocalypse were quickly moved to discount racks. Some were disappearing off bookstore shelves not because of the brisk sales they once enjoyed, but because they were being sent back to the publishers. Many of the Web sites containing disastrous predictions have either removed the articles or have shut down completely.

Dermot McGuigan, the coauthor of the survival guide *Y2K & Y-O-U,* first published in 1998, has since republished the book under its original name, *Your Resilient Home.* McGuigan said, "All the same information will be there, except the Y2K stuff will be played down."[33]

As we got closer to the year 2000, many of the prophets of doom were backpedaling. Some merely hedged their bets, reminding everyone that they only said "maybe" or that they never specified exactly what would happen. When the signs of the end became hazier, the declarations of "Apocalypse Now" by some prophets of doom slowly turned into "Apocalypse—Not Just Yet." "The end times people are backing down," said Damian Thompson, author of *The End of Time: Faith and Fear in the Shadow of the Millennium,* a study of modern doomsday cults. "People who last year became excited about the millennium bug are suddenly saying, 'I never said that. It was him, not me.' They're extremely nervous of having December 31, 1999, pinned on them forever."[34]

As church historian Tim Webber of Denver Seminary comments: "Whenever history takes one of its unexpected turns, the doomsayers end up with prophetic egg on their faces. But when their schemes don't fit anymore, you never see these folks owning up to it. They merely reshuffle [their dates] and come out with another edition [of predictions]."[35]

Earlier in 1999 the Reverend Jerry Falwell distributed a packet on "The Y2K Time Bomb," including a video advising people to be prepared for disaster, and a Family Readiness Checklist. "Y2K is God's instrument to shake this nation, to humble this nation," he said in a television broadcast. Yet Falwell said he was encouraged after reading the government's reports on Y2K. By December 1999 he predicted, "I don't anticipate any major problems."[36] By year's end, the video was no longer made available and Falwell had toned down his vision for 2000.

Grant Jeffery, author of *The Millennium Meltdown* and *Armageddon: Earth's Last Days,* was unmoved. Earlier Jeffrey predicted that the Y2K bug "may set the stage for the creation of the coming world government that was prophesied to arise in the last days." By late 1999, he downscaled his expectations. "It will be frustrating, like computer errors, delays in waiting for planes, that kind of thing. It's not a January problem. It will manifest itself gradually throughout the year, like maybe in March or April or May, or even later," he said.[37]

Michael Hyatt said in a January 3, 2000, press release that he was "cautiously optimistic." His primary analysis of the impact of Y2K put forward that "although the threat still remains, it does appear that the worst is past. However, I believe it is still too early to drop our guard."

Some of the doomsayers, however, were contrite if not totally repentant. Gary North said in February 2000, "I am certainly willing to say that my assessment of the threat, as things have played out, was incorrect. I did not think that fix-on-failure would work as well as a $500+ billion expenditure seems to have worked so far. I am indeed perplexed by the fact that those companies, nations, and local governments that spent almost nothing to fix Y2K seem to be performing as well as, say, Microsoft. Did I expect this? No."[38]

Among the repentant there were some who were all together disillusioned. In December 1997, Joe Boivin abandoned a promising career as the project manager at the Canadian Imperial Bank of Commerce to start, with his own funds, the first national program office for Y2K. Boivin founded the Global Millennium Foundation, an organization that publicized the threat of Y2K and sponsored industry and government efforts in Canada to tackle the problem.

The foundation's monthly online newsletter held an attitude of gloom and doom to the end. Even the last newsletter of 1999, published in November, stated, "The potential confusion at the turn of the century . . . continues to represent an explosive situation. Accidents and mistakes will continue to happen with ever greater frequency."

Now, however, Boivin feels like the Y2K problems were greatly overstated. "I have disqualified myself from giving any . . . advice," he said in January 2000. "The relief that a global crisis did not occur is tainted by a growing belief that there never was a global crisis, despite the multiple sources of confirmation reports. [It's] sort of like waking up one morning and discovering the Earth is flat."

He has since turned his attention to family matters, yet through it all Boivin says there is a lesson to be learned. "Y2K is an excellent example of how people from all parts of the world can come together for a common threat. [There's now] a better understanding of the interdependency of the world and the danger of allowing technology to become a life-threatening issue for entire nations." He also hailed "the coming together of competitors in similar industries to work together for a common cause."[39]

For many who were caught in the middle of the Y2K hype and predictions, the beginning of another new year was like a breath of fresh air. The world arose New Year's Day 2000 to find that "the trees and the sun and the clouds were all Y2K compliant," John Fiedler, minister at First United Methodist Church in Dallas, told his congregation. Christians should forget concerns about millennial disaster and "get back to the business of waging peace," he said.[40]

The time and energy spent on the Y2K computer problem

caused Christians to nearly miss "the sense that the return of Christ is imminent, and it's of far more importance than anything else," Rick VanWay, pastor of Church of the Nazarene in Beulah, N.D., said.[41]

At The Potter's House Church in Dallas, two caged lions were the featured attractions in a service. Bishop T. D. Jakes, pastor of the 24,000-member church explained that the animals represented the mighty power of God, and the fact that Christians should not fear but put their faith in the Almighty.

Borrowing the opening lines of Charles Dickens' novel *A Tale of Two Cities,* Billy Graham told Fox News Sunday, "I think it's going to be the best of times and the worst of times. I think this is exactly where we are right now, because we've now got the tools at our command to change the world for the better or for the worse."

Graham hoped that the future technological tools would help, not harm, humankind. "My fondest wish is that the Lord would come back and bring peace to the world because I'm deeply disturbed as I look into the future about all of this new technology that can destroy the human race."[42]

Sadly, there still seems to be division and hurt among those who took extraordinary precautions for Y2K and those who could say, "I told you so." The fallout from false predictions caused many good people to leave their churches and some leaders to leave their flocks—either by choice or prompted by those who accused them of not doing enough. Another tragedy in the wake of Y2K is the shame and disillusionment that many Christians feel for getting so excited about Y2K. In their earnestness to warn friends and family, many felt foolish when their words of warning failed to produce.

The truth is, God is not concerned about who is right and who is wrong. He is concerned about his people being rightly related to himself, his body—the church—and to the world. Now is the time for the members of the body of Christ to wrap their arms around one another, leave the past behind, and to move onward to a glorious future.

CHAPTER FIFTEEN

Onward Christian Soldiers

→ ←

For sale: powdered butter, broccoli, peas, and corn. Just add water, mix, and eat.

Gary Britt has been trying to sell $35,000 worth of survival food—enough to feed a family of four for seven years, or one person for thirty years.

You see Britt and five other families from a city east of Tampa, Florida, bought four hundred cases of dehydrated Y2K survival food over the Internet. It cost each family about $6,000. January 1, 2000, came and went without a glitch.

Now Britt hopes to recoup at least 75 percent of the money.

His classified add read: "Food, survival. 30 1-year units. 10-year shelf life. Price negotiable."[1]

Many churches across America formed Y2K committees to oversee the stocking of ample supplies in case the Y2K trouble really did come to pass. Like having a good fire insurance policy, many believers were hoping for the best but preparing for the worst. Preparedness is certainly a quality the Lord would approve of in his people. "For which one of you, when he wants to build a tower, does not first sit down and calculate the cost, to see if he has enough to complete it?" (Luke 14:28).

Many churches have sent their stored-up provisions overseas for mission use. Churches in areas that are prone to earthquakes or tornadoes continue to store some products in case of emergencies. If we learned anything from Y2K, it is to be prepared for all occasions, to be willing to share what we have with our communities, and to try to act responsibly before we meet the herald of the Judgment Day.

It's estimated that the United Sates spent more than any other country in the world—at least $100 billion—for software, hardware, services, and staff to make sure computers didn't crash at 12 A.M., January 1, 2000. Worldwide Y2K costs range from $280 billion to as much as $600 billion.

Interestingly, there was no one clamoring for people to prepare for the Apocalypse in much of the rest of the world. Yet the countries that so many experts felt were far behind in fixing Y2K weathered the rollover as well as the U.S. There was no selling of books, tapes, and survival gear. No one was suggesting that the year 2000 would bring an end to civilization, as we know it.

Was Y2K a giant hoax? Did the computer and government experts greatly exaggerate the possible fallout due to bugs in our software and worthless embedded chips in our cars, refrigerators, and VCRs? The answer is quite simply, no. There were some problems with computer-assisted equipment leading up to and after the year 2000 arrived. Nevertheless, Y2K seemed to be no more than a "bump in the road" for the most part.

FORGIVENESS—OF OURSELVES

Now that we are well past the year 2000, where do we go from here? First, we must learn to forgive—ourselves as well as others.

We must learn to forgive ourselves for being so vulnerable to every pronouncement of bad news. The gospel is still the "good news" that is able not only to save but to keep us in times of trouble. There are so many things clamoring for our attention today. Our lives are pulled in so many ways it's hard to discern the truth about life's circumstances.

We must walk in the light that the Lord has given us. To walk in darkness is to walk in deception, whether it comes from the world, the devil, or our flesh. Equally, to walk in the light is to walk in truth, by the Spirit of Truth. Instead of listening to every voice, we need to trust that still small voice that is inside each and every believer. It is his voice, through the Holy Spirit, our comforter, that will lead and guide us into all truth. "And I will ask the Father, and He will give you another Helper, that He may be with you forever; that is the Spirit of truth, whom the world cannot receive, because it does not behold Him or know Him, but you know Him because He abides with you, and will be in you" (John 14:16–17). "When the Helper comes, whom I will send to you from the Father, that is the Spirit of truth, who proceeds from the Father, He will bear witness of Me" (John 15:26).

Walking in truth creates right attitudes and builds right relationships, making us one with God and one with other like-minded members of the body of Christ.

The Lord in his lovingkindness has made us partakers of "the inheritance of the saints in light" (Col. 1:12). Darkness and deception no longer have authority over us because God has already "delivered us from the domain of darkness, and transferred us to the kingdom of His beloved Son" (Col. 1:13). For those who have wondered about the end times and the coming of the Lord, Paul foretells the suddenness of his coming:

> But of the times and the seasons, brethren, ye
> have no need that I write unto you.

For yourselves know perfectly that the day of
the Lord so cometh as a thief in the night.

For when they shall say, Peace and safety; then
sudden destruction cometh upon them, as travail
upon a woman with child; and they shall not
escape.

But ye, brethren, are not in darkness, that that
day should overtake you as a thief.

Ye are all the children of light, and the children of the day: we are not of the night, nor of
darkness. (1 Thess. 5:1–5 KJV)

If we truly are to be the children of the Light as Paul
describes, we must walk in the light and have no fellowship with
darkness at all. We have a divine mandate to "have no fellowship
with the unfruitful works of darkness, but rather reprove them"
(Eph. 5:11 KJV). In fact, Scripture is forceful in declaring, "Woe
to those who call evil good, and good evil; Who substitute darkness for light and light for darkness; Who substitute bitter for
sweet, and sweet for bitter! Woe to those who are wise in their
own eyes, and clever in their own sight" (Isa. 5:20–21).

Sin is darkness, and righteousness is light. Jesus is the Light of
all lights. He is the Unchanging One, for there is no shadow of
turning in him. We as individual lights have been made partakers
of his pure and radiant light. Our charge from heaven is to
become as unchanging in our stand during times of trouble as the
Lord himself. No wonder we are seen as a peculiar people to the
world, we who "proclaim the excellencies of Him who has called
you out of darkness into His marvelous light" (1 Pet. 2:9).

In John 9:5 Jesus said, "While I am in the world, I am the light
of the world," but in Matthew 5:14 he made this astonishing statement to His disciples: "You are the light of the world. A city set on
a hill cannot be hidden." Now that the Lord has ascended to the
right hand of the Father, the world can no longer see him, but
those who are called the joint heirs with Christ are now called to be

the light of the world. Because mankind must come to the light to be saved, Jesus commands all believers: "Let your light shine before men in such a way that they may see your good works, and glorify your Father who is in heaven" (Matt. 5:16).

Our lights point the way to the One who is the giver of life. To diminish this light in any way, or to cover it over, involves giving ground to darkness. Our gullibility to fall for legends, myths, superstitions, and false predictions can cause the Light of the World to appear dim. We must forgive ourselves for retreating from the Light in desperate time of trouble, and instead first seek the Lord and ask him to shine the light of truth over all that we hear, say, and do.

PREDICTIONS TO COME

We must also understand that there will always be those who believe they can predict future events. While some are very earnest in their desires, there are also those who will use the end times as a profitable venture. Sales of books, videos, and other items related to prophecy have continued well after the excitement of Y2K faded. Lots of industrious people found ways to make money selling real estate, portable home generators, how-to-books, and survival kits. Prophecy belief will always be a durable part of the American psyche, whether drawn from theological themes or in the infinite variations seeping into secular society. The end times as a growth industry demonstrates our desire to know and at least attempt to control the future. We must forgive those who hoped to profit from our vulnerability.

There were dozens of Christian media and church leaders who announced that Y2K was God's judgment on America and his wrath was yet to come. When nothing happened, several of these same prognosticators declared that God did a miracle and stopped the Y2K bug in its tracks. If their earlier declaration was that Y2K was the penalty for our sins as a nation, you might ask yourself, Are we more righteous now as a nation than a few years ago?

Some of the leaders who stated publicly that Y2K was God's anger toward America changed their minds after reading government and secular reports. One might ask if his wrath had been turned aside because of a government report. However, some doomsayers have stoically refigured the numbers, dating the time for the end to 2007, the end of the tribulation, 2033, counting from Christ's death instead of his birth.

FORGIVENESS OF OTHERS

We must forgive and love those who may have caused panic with their predictions. Love doesn't hold a grudge. It is by our love for one another that the world will know we are God's. Just as Paul encouraged the Colossians, we must encourage one another with this truth: "And so, as those who have been chosen of God, holy and beloved, put on a heart of compassion, kindness, humility, gentleness and patience; bearing with one another, and forgiving each other, whoever has a complaint against anyone; just as the Lord forgave you, so also should you. And beyond all these things put on love, which is the perfect bond of unity. And let the peace of Christ rule in your hearts, to which indeed you were called in one body; and be thankful" (Col. 3:12–15).

Yes, there will be those who want a "pound of flesh" or a stricter reign on leaders in the future, but first we must forgive. We must strive "with all humility and gentleness, with patience, showing forbearance to one another in love, being diligent to preserve the unity of the Spirit in the bond of peace" (Eph. 4:2–3). If the world is to be saved, they must see the church walking in unity. Jesus prayed in his High Priestly prayer of John 17:21 "that they may all be one; even as Thou, Father, art in Me, and I in Thee, that they also may be in Us; that the world may believe that Thou didst send Me."

LESSONS LEARNED

We must not only forgive, but we must now hold one another accountable. Paul pointed out that love would never fail, when we lovingly and purposefully hold ourselves answerable to each other. "Brethren, even if a man is caught in any trespass, you who are spiritual, restore such a one in a spirit of gentleness; looking to yourselves, lest you too be tempted. Bear one another's burdens, and thus fulfill the law of Christ. For if anyone thinks he is something when he is nothing, he deceives himself" (Gal. 6:1–3).

Jesus told us the reward we will receive for speaking the truth in love: "And if your brother sins, go and reprove him in private; if he listens to you, you have won your brother" (Matt. 18:15).

It demonstrates moral character when a leader will admit he is wrong. It takes even more courage and character for those who were offended to forgive and openly receive their offenders. But this demonstration of love is something the world is looking for. Those who made faulty predictions in the past must confess their sins to one another, and all of us need to pray for one another, so that we may be healed (James 5:16).

We can be confident that God is in the future and that the future is God's. We are not to be anxious about our lives, timid over tomorrow, or paralyzed with anxiety. There is an old adage that says, "If we worry, we won't trust, but if we trust, we won't worry." We must trust that the future is in God's hands and that what he says about it is the truth.

In today's secular psychotherapy, people in distress are encouraged to dig down, to draw from their resources within. Yet God urges us to press onward into the future with confidence, not a confidence in our abilities, but confidence in his power and grace. Even as Jesus moved toward the cross, he did not do it as One resigned to a hopeless fate, but as One confident that the future was glorious. He staked his life on that and, three days later, his trust was vindicated. Knowing that, we are able to move into the future with confidence, with powerful resources not of our own devising. This is good news. This is the truth.

APPENDIX

➤ ◄

Here is a partial list of computer virus hoaxes and some Web sites that provide information on current hoaxes and how to recognize them.

- *The Hoax Encyclopedia*—a resource list across the Web from *About.com:* <http://antivirus.about.com/compute/antivirus/library/blenhoax.htm>
- *Hoaxbusters*—The U.S. Dept. of Energy's clearinghouse for virus hoax information: <http://hoaxbusters.ciac.org/>
- *McAfee.com*—homepage of the maker of popular antivirus software: <http://mcafee.com/>
- *Symantic*—from the maker of Internet security technology: <http://www.symantec.com/avcenter/hoax.html>

EVOLVING LIST OF VIRUS HOAXES

- A.I.D.S. virus hoax
- An Internet flower for you
- AOL4FREE
- Baby New Year

- Badtimes
- Be My Valentine
- BUDDYLST.ZIP
- Budweiser frogs screen-saver scare
- California/Wobbler virus
- Elf Bowling
- Get more money
- Good Times
- Halloween
- Happy New Year
- Hotmail chain letter
- Let's watch TV virus
- Lump of Coal
- Mobile phone
- Phantom Menace
- PKZ300 Trojan
- Pokemon
- Returned or Unable to Deliver
- Sandman warning
- Teletubbies virus
- Ukraine/Despite
- Valentine's Greetings
- Win a Holiday
- Y2K7

NOTES

INTRODUCTION

1. Declan McCullagh, "What They Said with Dread," *Wired News.*
<http://www.wired.com/news/politics/0,1283,33419,00.html>

2. Ibid.

3. Ibid.

4. Mark A. Kellner, "Y2K: A Secular Apocalypse?" *Christianity Online* <http://www.christianityonline.com/ct/9t1/9t1054.html>

5. Alan E. Lewis, "Notable and Quotable," <http://gonow.to/y2kfacts>

6. Gary North, "Gary North's Y2K Links and Forums," <http://www.garynorth.com/y2k/detail.cfm/6577> October 10, 1999.

7. Richard Lacayo, "The End of the World As We Know It?" *Time.com* <http://www.time.com/time/digital/y2k/doom.html>

8. Charles Henderson, "Y2K Apocalypse Not," *About.Com.* <http://christianity.about.com/religion/christianity/library/weekly/aa122899.htm>

9. Ibid.

10. Kellner, "Y2K: A Secular Apocalypse."

11. Lacayo, "The End of the World As We Know It?"

12. Ibid.

13. Ibid.

14. Ibid.

15. Henderson, "Y2K Apocalypse Not."

16. Lacayo, "The End of the World As We Know It?"

17. Terasa Watanabe, "The Year of Believing Prophecies," *Los Angeles Times,* March 31, 1999.

18. Joel Stein Hey, "You in That Bunker, You Can Come Out Now!" *Time.com* <http://www.time.com/time/magazine/articles/0,3266, 36767,00.html>

1: LEGENDS IN OUR OWN MINDS

1. Teri Greene, "Don't Believe Those Wild Net Rumors," Gannett News Service, *USAToday.com,* <http://www.usatoday.com/life/cyber/tech/cti354.htm> August 7, 2000.

2. Barbara Mikkelson, "Gatored Community." *The Urban Legends References Pages* <http://www.snopes.com/critters/lurkers/gator.htm.

3. Associated Press, "As Net Grows, So Does the Number of Hoaxes," *Desert News,* <http://www.desnews.com/cgibin/libstory_reg?dn00&0003290083> March 29, 2000.

2: CHRISTIAN URBAN LEGENDS

1. William M. Alnor, *Soothsayer of the Second Advent* (Power Books, Fleming H. Revell Company, 1989), 77.

2. Mike Hutchinson, *First Baptist Church, Long Beach, MS* <http://www.fbclb.com/mike_hutchinson_update.htm> February 25, 2000.

3. James Wallace, "Flight 261 prayer story spreads via e-mail," *Seattle Post-Intelligencer,* http://www.seattlep-i.com/local/voic031.shtml> April 3, 2000.

4. Ibid.

5. Jan Harold Brunvand, *The Mexican Pet* (W. W. Norton, 1986), 175–77.

6. Barbara Mikkelson, "Gay Jesus Film," *The Urban Legends Research Pages,* <http://www.snopes.com/inboxer/petition/gayjesus.htm> April 21, 2000.

7. Alnor, *Soothsayer,* 74.

8. Rich Buhler, "The Beast of Belgium," *Ship of Fools,* <http://ship-of-fools.com/Myths/index.html> March 5, 2000.

9. Barbara Mikkelson, "Mark of the Devil," *The Urban Legends Reference Pages,* <http://www.snopes.com/spoons/fracture/barcode.htm> December 31, 1998.

10. Reuters, "New ID Cards Won't Carry Devilish 666," <http://home-news.excite.com/printstory/news/r/000407/07/odd-idcards> (April 7, 2000).

3: THE PETITION THAT WON'T GO AWAY

1. William J. Murray, *My Life without God* (Nashville: Thomas Nelson Publishers, 1982), 89.

2. Federal Communications Commission, "Religious Broadcasting Rumor Denied—Madalyn Murray O'Hair" <http://www.fcc.gov/mmb/enf/forms/rm-2493.html> February 5, 2000.

3. David Van Biema, "Where's Madalyn? The Missing Atheist Left Behind an Ailing Empire and a Trail of Tantalizing Clues," *ARACNET,* <http://www.aracnet.com/~atheism/writ/o'hairs10.htm> January 10, 2000.

4. William J. Murray, "Christian Testimony of William J. Murray," *William J. Murray Evangelistic Association,* <http://www.wjmurray.com/> March 9, 2000.

5. Doug Trouten, "Attack of the Fifty-Foot Hoax," *Charisma* magazine, April 1999.

6. Doug Trouten, "Have You Heard the One About," *Christian Coalition,* <http://www.cc.org/publications/ca/1196/hoax.html> November 29, 1999.

7. Trouten, "Have You Heard the One About," April 1, 2000.

8. Wyatt Andrews. "Pitfalls of the Digital Grapevine," *CBSNEWS. COM.* <http://cbsnews.cbs.com/now/story/0,1597,216674-412,00.shtml>

4: ENTERTAINING ANGELS

1. Billy Graham, *Angels: God's Secret Agents* (Doubleday and Company, 1975), 2.

2. Clete Hux, "Angelmania: Close Encounters of the Celestial Kind." *The Watchman Expositor.* <http://www.watchman.org/anglmani.htm>

3. Berit Kjos, "Touched by an Angel: But Which Kind?" *The Watchman Expositor.* <http://www.watchman.org/touchedbyangel.htm>

4. Ibid.

5. Terry Lynn Taylor, *Guardians of Hope: The Angels' Guide to Personal Growth* (H. J. Krammer, 1993).

6. Wendy Kaminer, "The Latest Fashion in Irrationality," *The Atlantic Monthly* <http://www.theatlantic.com/issues/96jul/angels/angels.htm> July 1996.

7. John Randolph Price, *Angel Energy: How to Harness the Power of Angels in Everyday Life* (Fawcett Books, 1995).

8. Doreen Virtue, *Healing with the Angels: How the Angels Can Assist You in Every Area of Your Life* (Hay House, 1999).

9. Nick Bunick, *In God's Truth* (Hampton Roads Publishing Co., 1998).

10. Dawn Raffel, "Angels All Around Us," *Redbook,* December 1992, 92.

11. Wendy Kaminer, "The Latest Fashion in Irrationality," *The Atlantic Monthly* <http://www.theatlantic.com/issues/96jul/angels/angels.htm> July 1996.

12. *The Detroit News,* "How to Know When You've Been Touched by an Angel," <http://detnews.com/menu/stories/23398.htm.> November 6, 1995.

13. James Redfield, *The Celestine Prophecy* (Warner Books, 1994).

5: BUSTING HELL WIDE OPEN

1. Rich Buhler, "Drilling for Hell," *Ship of Fools,* <http://ship-of-fools.com/Myths/03Myth.html> July 9, 1999.

2. Ibid.

3. Ibid.

6: THE MISSING DAY

1. Bert Thompson, "Has NASA Discovered Joshua's 'Lost Day'?" *Apologetics Press,* <http://www.apologeticspress.org/> February 1999.

2. Ibid.

3. Richard Riss, "Christian Evidences: The Long Day of Joshua," *Richard M. Riss Homepage* <http://www.grmi.org/renewal/Richard_Riss/evidences/7longday.html>

4. Thompson, "Has NASA Discovered Joshua's 'Lost Day'?"

5. "The Day the Earth Stood Still," *The Urban Legends Research Centre* <http://www.ulrc.com.au/> April 10, 2000.

7: AS SEEN ON TV

1. Barbara Mikkelson, "(trade) Mark of the Devil," *The Urban Legends Reference Pages* <http://www.snopes.com/spoons/legends/procter.htm> August 12, 1999.

2. "Corporate Facts," *Tommy.com,* <http://www.tommy.com/help/faq_corporate_facts.jhtml#rumors> August 2000.

8: BE AFRAID. BE VERY AFRAID

1. "Are These Stories True?" *Centers for Disease Control and Prevention Update* <http://www.cdc.gov/nchstp/hiv_aids/pubs/faq/faq5a.htm> November 30, 1998.

2. "Frequently Asked Questions," *Burger King Corporation* <http://www.burgerking.com/company/e-mail.htm> October 23, 1998.

3. David Emery, "Return of the 'Blue Star' LSD. Tattoo," *Urban Legends and Folklore—About.com* <http://urbanlegends.miningco.com/

culture/urbanlegends/library/weekly/aa102198.htm> October 21, 1998.

4. Jan Harold Brunvand, *The Choking Doberman and Other New Urban Legends* (New York: W. W. Norton & Company Inc., 1984).

5. Dave Gross, "What is the 'Blue Star' LSD Tattoo urban legend," *The "Blue Star" LSD Tattoo Urban Legend Page* <http://users.lycaeum. org/~sputnik/tattoo> February 3, 2000.

6. Paul Hartwell, "Flash Your Lights and Die," *Urban Legends and Folklore—About.com.* <http://urbanlegends.about.com/science/urban legends/library/blbyol16.htm> November 20, 1997.

7. "False Internet Report about Bananas," *Centers for Disease Control and Prevention,* <http://www.cdc.gov/ncidod/banana.htm> February 10, 2000.

8. John Bartlett, comp. (1820–1905), "Familiar Quotations 9th ed. 1901," *Bartleby.com* <http://www.bartleby.com/index.html>

9. Jan Harold Brunvand, *Too Good To Be True* (W. W. Norton & Company, 1999), 26.

9: THE MISINFORMATION AGE

1. "Make-A-Wish Foundation Does Not Participate in Chain Letter or Other Direct Solicitation Wishes," *Make-A-Wish Foundation® of America* <http://www.wish.org/home/frame_chainletters.htm.> April 5, 2000.

2. *American Cancer Society* <http://www.cancer.org/letter.html> March 29, 2000.

3. Barbara Mikkleson, "Thousand Dollar Bill," *The Urban Legends Reference Pages,* <http://www.snopes.com/inboxer/nothing/billgate. htm> March 30, 2000.

4. Patrick Crispen, "Now That Microsoft and AOL Have Merged, Is Microsoft Really Going to Pay You for Forwarding an E-mail to All of Your Friends?" *Urban Legend Combat Page* <http://www.netsquirrel. com/combatkit/e-mailforward.html> April 28, 2000.

5. Lynn Burke, "This 'Virus' Is an Apparition," *Wired News* <http://www.wired.com/news/culture/0,1284,35465,00.html> April 10, 2000.

6. *U.S. Department of Energy Computer Incident Advisory Capability* <http://www.ciac.org/> April 1, 2000.

7. "Electronic Greeting Cards Are Safe; Blue Mountain and Symantec Expose Virus Hoax," *Symantec Corporation* <http://www. symantec.com/press/1999/n990311b.html.> March 11, 1999.

8. Robert Lemos, "Inside the 'ILOVEYOU' worm," *ZDNN,* <http: //www.zdnet.com/zdnn/stories/news/0,4586,2562483,00.html> May 4, 2000.

10: THE EXPERTS SPEAK

1. *The Kansan Online* <http://celebrate2000.thekansan.com/stories/042099/nex_predictions.shtml> April 20, 1999.

11: MILLENNIUM FEVER

1. Stephen D. O'Leary, "Who's Afraid of the Millennium?" *Microsoft® Encarta® Online Encyclopedia 2000* <http://encarta.msn.com> May 1, 2000.
2. "What Really Happened in 1000 A.D.? Part I," *Uncle John's Indispensable Guide to the Year 2000* (The Bathroom Readers Press, 1998).
3. O'Leary, "Who's Afraid of the Millennium?"
4. Damian Thompson, *The End of Time: Faith and Fear in the Shadow of the Millennium* (University Press of New England, 1996), 29.
5. William M. Alnor, *Soothsayers of the Second Advent* (Power Books, Fleming H. Revell Company, 1989), 106.
6. Thompson, *The End of Time*.
7. "Why We Must Reject Millennium Madness," *Charisma and Christian Life* <http://www.charismamag.com/articledisplay.pl/?d=cm7991&MonthID=cm799>
8. Ron Rhodes, "Millennium Madness," *Reasoning from the Scriptures Ministries* <http://home.earthlink.net/~ronrhodes/MilMad.html>
9. Alnor, *Soothsayers of the Second Advent*, 102.
10. Ibid.
11. Mark A. Kellner, "Y2K: A Secular Apocalypse?" *Christianity Online* <http://www.christianityonline.com/ct/9t1/9t1054.html>
12. Ibid.
13. Stephen Jay Gould, *Questioning the Millennium* (New York: Harmony Books, 1997), 106–107.
14. Ibid.

12: THE END OF THE WORLD

1. "Chronological Index of Last Days Mis-Prophecies," *Erala Home Page* <http://www.geocities.com/Athens/Acropolis/5766/prophecies.html>
2. "Why We Must Reject Millennium Madness," *Charisma and Christian Life* <http://www.charismamag.com/articledisplay.pl/?d=cm7991&MonthID=cm799> July 1999.
3. Damian Thompson, *The End of Time: Faith and Fear in the Shadow of the Millennium* (University Press of New England, 1996), 30.
4. "Chronological Index of Last Days Mis-Prophecies."
5. C. Marvin Pate and Calvin B Haines Jr., *Doomsday Delusions* (InterVarsity Press, 1995), 87.

6. "Chronological Index of Last Days Mis-Prophecies."

7. Otto Friedrich, *The End of the World: A History* (Coward, McCann & Geoghegan, 1986).

8. B. J. Oropeza and Hank Hanegraaff, *99 Reasons Why No One Knows When Christ Will Return* (InterVarsity Press, 1994).

9. Eugen Weber, *Apocalypses* (Harvard University Press, 1999).

10. Thompson, *The End of Time.*

11. William M. Alnor, *Soothsayer of the Second Advent* (Power Books, Fleming H. Revell Company, 1989), 58.

12. Watchtower Bible and Tract Society, *The Watchtower,* October 15, 1958, 613.

13. Hal Lindsey, C. C. Carlson, *The Late Great Planet Earth* (Zondervan Publishing, 1970), 43.

14. Quoted in Samuele Bacchiocchi, "Hal Lindsey's Prophetic Jigsaw Puzzle: Five Predictions That Failed," <http://www2.andrews.edu/~samuele/books/jigsaw_puzzle/1.html>

15. Ibid.

16. Chris Hall, "What Hal Lindsey Taught Me about the Second Coming," *Christianity Online* <http://www.christianityonline.com/ct/9tc/9tc082.html> October 25, 1999.

17. Alnor, *Soothsayers of the Second Advent.*

18. Hall, "What Hal Lindsey Taught Me about the Second Coming."

19. Edgar C Whisenant, *88 Reasons Why the Rapture Will Be in 1988* (Nashville, TN: World Bible Society, 1988).

20. Alnor, *Soothsayers of the Second Advent.*

21. Edgar Whisenant and Greg Brewer, *The Final Shout: Rapture Report 1989* (Nashville, TN: World Bible Society, 1989).

22. Ibid., 6.

23. Ibid.

24. Ibid., 81.

25. Harold Camping, (New York: Vantage Press, 1992, 1994?).

26. Robert Sungenis, Scott Temple, and David Allen Lewis *Shock Wave 2000! Harold Camping's 1994 Debacle* (Green Forest, AZ: New Leaf Press, 1994).

27. "Timeline of Apocalyptic Prediction," *Center for Millennial Studies* <http://www.linternet.com/projects/cms/timeline/>

28. B. J. Oropeza, "One More End-Time Scare Ends with a Whimper," *Christian Research Journal,* <http://www.iclnet.org/pub/resources/text/cri/cri-jrnl/crj0122a.txt> (Winter 1993).

29. Ibid.

30. Terasa Watanabe, "Millennium Madness," *Los Angeles Times,* March 31, 1999.

31. Alnor, *Soothsayers,* 32.

32. Ibid.

33. Jack Taylor, *The Word of God with Power* (Broadman & Holman Publishers, 1993), 158.

13: WILL THE REAL ANTICHRIST PLEASE STAND UP

1. "A Magick Life. A Biography of Aleister Crowle," *Mail on Sunday,* <http://beta.yellowbrix.com/pages/newsreal/Story.nsp?story_id=12645993&ID=newsreal&scategory=AP+Top+Headlines>

2. Robert Fuller, *Naming the Antichrist: The History of an American Obsession* (New York, Oxford: Oxford University Press, 1995), 161.

3. William M. Alnor, *Soothsayer of the Second Advent* (Power Books, Fleming H. Revell Company, 1989), 139.

4. Ibid., 24.

5. Ibid.

6. Ibid., 141.

7. "True Parents" *The Unification Church* <http://unification.org/>

8. Alnor, *Soothsayer,* 197.

14: Y2K—THE BUG THAT DIDN'T BITE

1. Declan McCullagh, "The Year We Noticed Y2K," *Wired News* <http://www.wired.com/news/culture/0,1284,17093,00.html> December 31, 1998.

2. Declan McCullagh, "The Bug Inside the Beltway," *Wired News* <http://www.wired.com/news/y2k/0,1360,19265,00.html> April 22, 1999.

3. David Snyder, "Y2K Forecasts," Christian Broadcasting Network, *CBN.com* <<http://www.cbnnow.com/newsstand/stories/990720.asp> July 20, 1999.

4. Ibid.

5. David McGuire, "Only 3 States Y2K Ready," *ComputerUser.com* <http://currents.net/newstoday/99/08/18/news15.html>

6. Robert Burns, "U.S. Military Ready for Y2K," The Associated Press, *ABC News* <http://abcnews.go.com/ABC2000/abc2000us/y2k_pentagon991216.html> 1999.

7. Robert Rankin, "2000 Reasons to Worry," Mercury News Washington Bureau, *SiliconValley.com* <http://www.mercurycenter.com/svtech/news/indepth/docs/y2k092299.htm> September 21, 1999.

8. Stephen Barr, "House Holds Final 1999 Y2K Hearing," *WashingtonPost.com* <http://washingtonpost.com/wp-srv/WPlate/1999-11/05/111l-110599-idx.html> November 5, 1999.

9. Declan McCullagh, "What They Said with Dread," *Wired News* <http://www.wired.com/news> January 4, 2000.

10. Ibid.

11. Ibid.

12. Gary North, "The Year 2000 Problem: The Year the Earth Stands Still," *Gary North's Y2K Links and Forums* <http://www.garynorth.com> October 20, 1999.

13. Ira Rifkin, "Christian Conservatives divided on Y2K hoopla," *Religion News Service* November 13, 1999).

14. "Why We Must Reject Millennium Madness," *Charisma and Christian Life* <http://www.charismamag.com/articledisplay.pl/?d=cm7991&MonthID=cm799>

15. "Y2K: The World Wide Computer Crash," *Religion Today, Crosswalk.com* <http://www.religiontoday.com/Archive/FeatureStory/view.cgi?file=19980917.s1.html>

16. John Alderman, "Y2K: A Novel Approach," *Wired News* <http://www.wired.com/news/culture/0,1284,14493,00.html> August 19, 1998.

17. Mark A. Kellner, "Y2K: A Secular Apocalypse?" *Christianity Online* <http://www.christianityonline.com/ct/9t1/9t1054.html>

18. McCullagh, "What They Said with Dread."

19. Steve Hewitt, "Editorial: I Am Distressed over Christian Reporting on Y2K," *Christian Computing* magazine <http://www1.gospelcom.net/ccmag/y2k/edit1098.html> October 1998.

20. "Y2K: The World Wide Computer Crash."

21. Richard Lacayo, "The End of the World As We Know It?" *Time.com* <http://www.time.com/time/digital/y2k/doom.html>

22. Ibid.

23. Steve Hewitt, "Don't Be Ashamed If You Hold a Moderate Position on Y2K," *Christian Computing* <http://www.gospelcom.net/ccmag/>

24. Lacayo, "The End of the World As We Know It?"

25. Associated Press, "Christian Group Fears Computer Bug," *@Home Network,* April 3, 1999.

26. Steve Hewitt, "Don't Be Ashamed If You Hold a Moderate Position on Y2K."

27. Ibid.

28. Ibid.

29. Kellner, "Y2K: A Secular Apocalypse?"

30. Ibid.

31. Ibid.

32. Art Levine, "Confessions of a (Former) Y2K Paranoid," *The American Prospect Online* <http://www.prospect.org/webarchives/00-01/levine.html> January 6, 2000.

33. Associated Press, "Y2K Bug Book to Be Revamped," *@Home Network* January 5, 2000.

34. Hanna Rosin, "As January 1 Draws Near, Doomsayers

Reconsider," *WashingtonPost.com* <http://washingtonpost.com/wp-srv/WPlate/1999-12/27/0671-122799-idx.html> December 27,1999.

35. "Why We Must Reject Millennium Madness."
36. Charles Henderson, "Y2K Apocalypse Not," *About.Com.* <http://christianity.about.com/religion/christianity/library/weekly/aa1 22899.htm>
37. Rosin, "As January 1 Draws Near, Doomsayers Reconsider."
38. Gary North, "Declan McCullagh Calls for Repentance from Y2K Alarmists," *Gary North's Y2K Links and Forums* <http://www.gary north.com/y2k/detail_.cfm/7104> January 5, 2000.
39. Gary H. Anthes, "Y2K Prophet Comes Down from Soapbox," *Computer World* <http://www.computerworld.com/home/print.nsf/all/000117E082> January 17, 2000.
40. "Press Onward Christian Leaders Say," *Religion Today, Crosswalk.com* <http://www.religiontoday.com/Archive/FeatureStory/view.cgi?file=20000104.s1.html>
41. Ibid.
42. Ibid.

15: ONWARD CHRISTIAN SOLDIERS

1. "Survival Food on the Market," Associated Press, *Edmond Evening Sun* (Edmond, OK), August 13, 2000.

**For more information about John A. Williams
and Sound of His Voice Ministry:**

**Box 5524
Edmond, Oklahoma 73013-5524
405-478-7911
costofdeception@yahoo.com**